APPROACHES TO SEMIOTICS

edited by

THOMAS A. SEBEOK

assisted by

DONNA JEAN UMIKER

31

HANDBOOK OF GESTURES:

COLOMBIA AND THE UNITED STATES

by

ROBERT L. SAITZ
Associate Professor of English
Boston University

EDWARD J. CERVENKA
Consultant in Applied Linguistics
New York City

with illustrations by

MEL PEKARSKY
New York City

1972

MOUTON

THE HAGUE · PARIS

© Copyright 1972 in The Netherlands
Mouton & Co. N.V., Publishers, The Hague.

No part of this book may be translated or reproduced in any form, by print, photoprint, microfilm, or any other means, without written permission from the publishers.

Printed in The Netherlands

ACKNOWLEDGEMENTS

For help in the preparation of this second edition, the authors wish to gratefully acknowledge the generous financial assistance provided by the Faculty Research Fund of Teachers College, Columbia University and the Graduate School of Boston University.

We wish also to thank all the readers who have so kindly sent us comments on the first edition. Finally, we would like to acknowledge the assistance of Dorothy A. Ludwig for helping with the bibliography, Miryam Morin for critical comments, and Jennifer Monson for preparation of the index and typing of the final manuscript.

R. L. S. E. J. C.
Stoneham, Mass. New York City

INTRODUCTION

> We respond to gestures with an extreme alertness and one might almost say, in accordance with an elaborate code that is written nowhere, known by none, and understood by all.
> Edward Sapir

This handbook of Colombian and U.S. gestures derived originally from the experience of the authors during their terms as Fulbright lecturers in Columbia, 1960 to 1962. After a first impression that Colombians used body movements as an accompaniment to and sometimes as a substitute for verbal communication much more frequently than people from the U.S., we began to observe gestures more systematically and soon noted that many gestures were the same in physical movement and meaning for Colombians and for people from the U.S. while other gestures seemed unique to each group, and still others were the same in physical movement for each group but different in meaning. It was the gestures in the last category, whose misinterpretation could so easily lead to misunderstanding (e.g. a lecturer from the U.S. was discussing the stages of language learning and when he said that children of five already control a good deal of their native language, his Colombian audience laughed; his gesture for indicating the height of the children had been arm extended with palm facing down, and in Colombia this gesture is used when referring to the size of animals, not humans), that led us to prepare an inventory of the more obvious gestures used by Colombians and people from the U.S. as an aid to the English teachers with whom we were working.

We collected the gestures of the Colombians on the basis of personal observations in Colombia during 1960-1962 and from interviews with Colombian informants during that same period. The interviews with the Columbian informants, two male and two female took place over a period of twelve months and consisted of (1) our presentation of observed gestures for their recognition and comment, and (2) discussion and simulation of varied contexts in an attempt to elicit further gestures. During the same period and afterwards, some twenty informants, male and female, from different regions of the U.S., were interviewed by the same procedures. To the gestures collected and published in 1962, we have added others for this edition, collected through our own observation and through the response of readers to the initial publication. The informants in Colombia were young-adult and middle-aged, and came from Bogota and Tunja (though our observations were made in a number of other cities and towns of Colombia as well). The informants from the U.S. represented a wide range of ages and of geographical and social backgrounds. And although it was not possible to conduct representational or random sample surveys or to investigate case histories in sufficient depth to accumulate sociolinguistic data, the information we were able to collect on age and class variations (noted in the descriptions of some of the gestures) suggests that further research will reveal significant sociolinguistic patterns.

Recognition that gestures, body stance, body positioning, touching, etc. constitute an important part of communication has led to a variety of investigations of such phenomena, particularly during the last few decades. Ray Birdwhistell's work on the description of the kinesic behavior of individuals and of communities, D. Efron's characterization of culturally different configurations of emphasis, the studies of Paul Ekman, Wallace Friesen, A.E. Scheflen, and others on the roles which observation of kinesic behavior can play in psychotherapy, represent some of the directions of these investigations (we have listed a representative number of such studies in our bibliography).

This study, which originated in an effort to point out some of the more obvious gestural differences between cultures to a group of language teachers, focuses on gestures which (1) seem discrete (that is they have an essential physical movement which, imformants agree, characterizes the gesture), and (2) are easily recognizable by an untrained observer. Actually, of course, most of what we here call gestures are complexes of motion, analogous perhaps to the larger units of linguistic communication, such as the sentence, which are capable of being analyzed further into discrete components (see the work of Birdwhistell, for example). Our purpose in using the larger unit recognized as 'gesture' here has been to collect a corpus or foci, to gather together as many gesture complexes as possible and to designate them with a broad semantic label (which calls attention to an area of meaning that the complex be associated with), as a stimulus to further research. We have excluded, for the most part, some specialized gesture systems which merit collection and study: (1) the difficult to see (but certainly significant) changes in pupil openings, and in the movement of minute facial muscles; (2) ritual gesture systems used within relatively closed groups (church, army, sports, secret organizations, crane operators, etc.); (3) deaf and dumb systems; (4) children's game gestures; (5) heavily iconic gestures (a child's imitation of driving a car, a finger rubbing teeth to denote brushing teeth, fingers closing to depict a scissors, etc.); (6) stage gestures; (7)

paralanguage. Nor have we attempted to describe total body configurations which at times characterize communities and regions (i.e. the round-shouldered stoop pattern, the belly-forward, hands in pocket/belt slouch, etc.). Although we refer to and note some of the above categories in the text, we include primarily adult gestures recognizable by informants as message carriers or verbal message accompaniers.

Our collection here is, of course, far from complete. The nature of gesture and the difficulty of gesture elicitation guarantee this. Gestures are almost always used unconsciously—most people are surprised when they see how much they do gesture (as in a film). Further, gesturing is often not considered socially attractive; many informants deny any use of gesture. Finally, many gestures occur infrequently (they are like infrequent lexical items, but unlike lexical items they have not been recorded, or frozen, in texts). Even if one were to adopt an exhaustively descriptive technique and film the movements of representative members of a community over a two year period, he would probably record only a small proportion of the gesture inventory of the community.[1] Thus, although we have recorded here some gestures, we know the handbook is far from complete and we welcome communications from readers with comments on entries and information on unrecorded gestures.

The gestures in the handbook have been labelled semantically. But the description of the meaning of gestures presents us with a problem similar to that of the lexicographer. Gestures, somewhat like words, are not self-contained; they are one kind of behavior, which other kinds to help shape the total meaning of a communication. They have their meaning only within the total context, and thus any cataloguing, which pulls them out of context, is arbitrary and somewhat unsatisfactory.[2] We have used the semantic label because of its broadness, because it points to a total context rather to a part of a message. Our semantic labels range from the very general (ANGER) to the specific (THIEF), reflecting the kinds of meaning carried by gestures. For example, just as a word or utterance in verbal communication, a gesture or gestural pattern may carry a meaning which is not too closely dependent upon the observer's knowledge of the background of the performer or the context of the gesture (Thus the use of the VICTORY gesture (a V made by index and middle fingers) gives the observer a specific meaning at once, though of course the significance of the victory depends on context). On the other hand, gestures labelled under THOUGHT take almost all their meaning from the circumstances of the context.

In addition to the semantic labelling, which is alphabetical, we have described the gestures in non-technical language and we have illustrated them. Although

---

1. In-depth interviews with as wide a range of informants as possible seems a more promising approach.
2. Unless it were one so exhaustive as to be unreadable, as has happened with both the compendium and the distinctive semantic feature kinds of description.

ideally we might have liked slow-motion photography of each gesture and its contexts, we chose graphic illustration because of the nature of the handbook, an inventory which is designed as a stimulus to the collection of a greater inventory. In such circumstances, we deemed easy recognition and easy availability as the prime desiderata, and drawings, which capture the essence of the movement, which are easily recognizable, and which can be easily reproduced, seemed appropriate.

The gestures have been further labelled in the text to indicate similarities and differences in Columbian and U.S. gestures.[3] In such a comparison of the gesture systems of two cultures, there are possibilities of (1) the same, or very similar, meaning represented by the same gesture; (2) the same meaning represented by different gestures; (3) the same gestures representing a different meaning in each culture, and (4) a unique-gesture-meaning in each culture. To denote condition (1) we have used the designation COMMON; for the other three categories we merely indicate whether the gesture is Colombian or U.S., except that for category (3) we have added to the country designations the label AMBIGUOUS. Descriptions of the gestures also include sample accompanying phrases when these seem particularly frequent or useful to the teacher or language student.

In this edition, we also present tables of content in English and Spanish, an index which lists the semantic labels plus other content words from the descriptions which might aid a reader in locating a gesture, and finally a selective bibliography.

---

3. A number of the gestures in this text are common of course in other cultures as well; others are similar (*THIN*, for example is made in parts of Italy with the forefinger), and still others are quite different (*APPROVAL* A: same movements in Sicily mean 'I don't care how badly you want it, you're not getting it.').

TABLE OF CONTENTS

Acknowledgements		5
Introduction		7
Agreement	(Acuerdo)	15
Anger	(Ira)	16
Anticipation	(Anticipo)	17
Approval	(Aceptacion)	19
Attention	(Atencion)	21
Aversion	(Aversion)	23
Baby		24
Bet	(Apuesta)	24
Boredom	(Aburrimiento)	25
Cigarette	(Cigarrillo)	25
Cold	(Frio)	26
Come	(Ven, venga)	27
Complication	(Enredo)	29
Cross	(Cruz)	29
Crowd	(Multitúd)	30
Dance (invitation)	(Baile - invitacion)	30
Delicacy	(Finura, delicadeza)	31
Denial	(Negacion)	32
Directions	(Direcciones)	33
Disagreement	(Desacuerdo)	36
Disappointment	(Contrariedád)	37
Disapproval	(Reprobár)	38
Disbelief	(Incredulidád)	39
Disgust	(Fastidio)	43
Disinterest	(Desinterés)	43
Drink	(Tomár)	44
Drunk	(Borracho)	45
Emphasis	(Enfasis - en la conversacion	46
Encouragement	(Animár, dar ánimo)	48
Enthusiasm	(Entusiasmo)	49
Excitement	(Excitár)	50
Fat	(Gordiflón [na], gruesco [sa]	51
Faux Pas	(Errór- darse cuenta	51

TABLE OF CONTENTS

Favor	(Favór, ayuda)	53
Female	(Mujér)	54
Fight	(Riña, pelea)	54
Flirtation (wink)	(Coqueteo, [guiño]	55
Following	(Atrás, detrás)	55
Food	(Comida)	56
Friendship	(Amistád)	57
Frustration	(Frustracĭon)	58
Full	(Lleno)	58
Go (Traffic Direction)	(Pasen-Señales de tránsito)	59
Goad	(Meter cizaña)	60
Goodbye	(Adiós)	61
Gossip	(Murmuracĭon)	64
Graft	(Soborno)	64
Greetings	(Saludos)	65
Height	(Estatura)	70
Hitchhiking	(Pasaje - gratuito - pedirlo gratuitamente en la carretera)	70
Hot	(Calór)	71
Impatience	(Impaciencia)	73
Imprisonment	(Encarcelár)	74
Insanity	(Demencia)	75
Insults	(Insulto)	76
Intelligence	(Inteligencia)	78
Kiss	(Beso)	79
Leave	(Despedida)	80
Luck	(Suerte)	82
Marriage	(Matrimonio)	84
Masculinity	(Hombria - machismo)	85
Memory	(Memoria)	86
Money	(Dinero, plata)	88
More or Less	(Más o menos)	91
Nervousness	(Nerviosidád, intranquilidád, inquietúd)	92
No Information	(No sé)	92
Oath	(Juramento)	94
Perfection	(Perfeccĭon)	95
Photograph	(Fotografiár, ftografia)	95
Pride	(Orgullo)	96
Proximity & Touching	(Distancia y toque - corporál)	97
Punishment	(Castigo)	98
Quickly	(Rápido)	99
Recognition	(Reconocimiento, gratitúd)	99
Regret, chagrin	(Arrepentimiento, pesár)	100
Repetition	(Repeticĭon)	103
Requests	(Pedĭr)	104
Restaurant Gestures	(Restaurante - gestos que ocurren en uno)	106
Retribution	(Propina, gratificacĭon)	111
Revenge	(Desquite, venganza, represalia)	111
Review	(Repasár)	112
Saintliness	(Santidád)	112
Self (me)	(Yo - mismo)	113
Sexual gestures	(Sexo)	114

TABLE OF CONTENTS 13

Shame	(Vergüenza)	123
Silence	(Silencio)	123
Sit	(Sentár)	124
Sleep	(Dormír)	125
Slow down (traffic)	(Disminuïer - la velocidád)	126
Small	(Pequeño)	126
Smell	(Olór, hedór)	127
Snobbishness	("Snobismo")	128
Stand	(Parár)	129
Stinginess	(Tacañeria)	129
Stop	(Pare)	130
Strength	(Fortaleza)	132
Success	(Éxito)	134
Surprise	(Sorpresa)	134
Talk	(Hablár)	136
Telephone	(Teléfono)	136
Termination	(Termine, fin)	137
Thief	(Ladrón)	138
Thin	(Delgado -a, flaco -a)	139
Threat		142
Time	(Tiempo)	143
Tiredness	(Cansancio)	144
Victory	(Victoria, triunfo)	145
Wait	(Esperár)	146
Warning	(Advertír)	147
What ?	(Como ? Qúe ?)	149
What happened ?	(Que pasó ?)	150
Yes/No	(Si/No)	151
Bibliography		153
Word Index		163

AGREEMENT
A.

COL.   Vigorous hand clasp.

AGREEMENT
B.

COMMON.   Head nods up and down. Many variations: e.g. eyebrows raised, eyes open, head nodding rapidly for an enthusiastic agreement; head nodding slowly, corners of mouth drawn for a grudging assent, etc.

I agree with you.   De acuerdo.

ANGER
A.

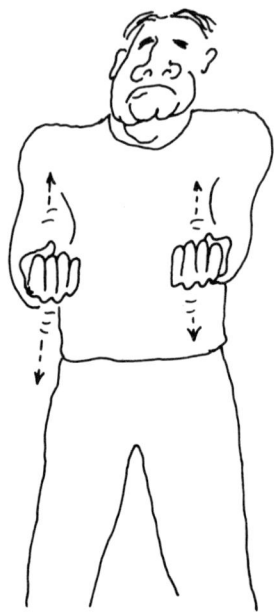

COL.   Forearms are extended in front of body, parallel to ground; hands are made into fists. Fists make a short, sharp downward, then upward motion.

ANGER
B.

COMMON.   Fist is shaken vigorously.

ANGER
C.

COMMON.   Fists held together and twisted as if wringing a cloth.

ANGER A, B, C can also indicate threats and fights. See FIGHT (p. 54).

ANTICIPATION
A.

COMMON.   Hands, palm to palm, are rubbed together briskly.

ANTICIPATION
B.

COMMON. Tongue extended about a quarter of an inch, moves slowly along width of lips. Eyes widen.

ANTICIPATION
C.

U.S. Hands are held palm to palm, or clasped in front of the body. Female.
ANTICIPATION gestures may also be used to indicate APPROVAL.

APPROVAL
A.

(1) (2)

COL. Index finger touches skin just below eye. Sometimes eye is opened wider by spulling the skin below the eye downward. Used frequently to refer to members of the opposite sex.

Wonderful, beautiful, etc.   Good looking.
Qúe bueno, guapo, etc.

APPROVAL
B.

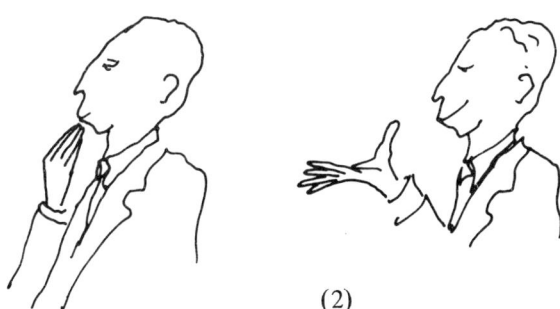

(1) (2)

COL. Fingers of one hand come to a point and press against lips. Hand then moves quickly and opens with fingers spreading. Used more frequently by men. A dramatic gesture which can refer to a person or an object.

Wonderful, beautiful, tasty, sexually attractive, etc.
Guapa, sabrosa, exquisita, etc.

APPROVAL
C.

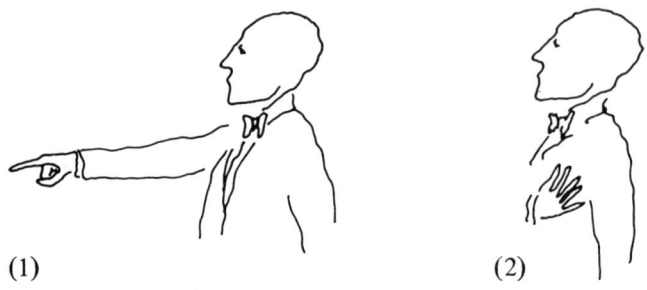

(1) (2)

COL.   Extended index finger is pointed at referent; then hand is placed on chest.

I like (or love) you, her, etc.
La, te, etc. quiero.

APPROVAL
D.

COMMON.   Eye wink. Mostly a male gesture in both cultures. Depending on the context, this gesture ranges in meaning from accord to approbation to invitation.

See FLIRTATION (p. 55).

APPROVAL (APPLAUSE)

E.

COMMON.   Hand Clapping.

> See ANTICIPATION and PERFECTION for other gestures of approval.

ATTENTION

A.

(1)

COL.   Performer points his index finger to his eye and then to object being indicated. (1) May occur alone.

ATTENTION
B.

COL.   Hand raised, finger extended. Common classroom gesture.

ATTENTION
C.

COMMON.   Hand extended with fingers together. Common U.S. classroom gesture — in Colombia it alternates with ATTENTION B. When a U.S. student is especially eager for attention, he will wave his arm from side to side; the Colombian student will more frequently thrust his arm forward repeatedly under similar circumstances.

ATTENTION
D.

COMMON. Neighbor is nudged with elbow. This gesture in both cultures is proper only with close friends; with orders it would be impolite.

Look. Mira.

AVERSION

COMMON. Eyes are directed away from the face or person being spoken to. Eyes may stare into space, at an object, or at the ground.

24   HANDBOOK OF GESTURES

BABY

    COMMON.   Hands and arms make a motion as if holding a baby and move from side to side, as if rocking a baby to sleep.

BET
  A.

    COL.   The bettors link little fingers. At times one may strike the linked fingers with his free hand.

BET
  B.

    COMMON.   A Handshake.

BOREDOM

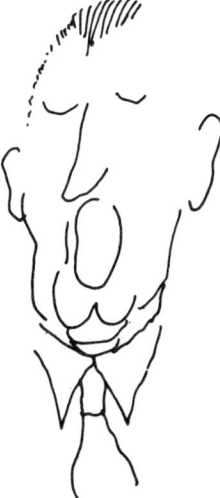

COMMON. While the yawn may be involuntary, it can also be used deliberately (for example, as a signal that one is bored at a party or performance and wants to leave).

See IMPATIENCE C and NERVOUSNESS (pp. 74, 92).

CIGARETTE

COMMON. Index and middle fingers form V in front of lips. Sometimes they touch the lips; sometimes they are brought together as they touch the lips. Normally a request for a cigarette, this gesture was observed in Colombia with the additional meaning of *your car is smoking, burning.*

COLD

A.

COMMON. Hands, palm to palm, are rubbed together vigorously. Shoulders are hunched. Often accompanied by sound *brrrrrr* in U.S.

COLD

B.

COMMON. Each hand grasps opposite upper arm as shoulders are hunched.

Many Colombians, especially in the cool, highland regions, cover their noses and mouths with handkerchief when going out into the night air, e.g. when leaving theaters, homes, etc. The custom rests upon the belief that the change of temperature from inside to outside is harmful; for this reason also, it is common to find delayed goodbyes at the front door, with the door open, as the departing guests accustom themselves to the outside air.

HANDBOOK OF GESTURES 27

COME

A.

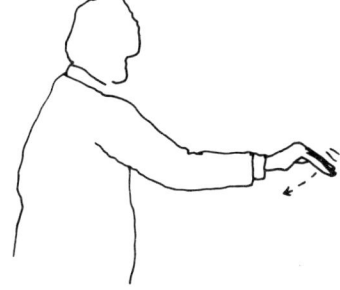

Ambiguous. Palm faces away from face as fingers move back and forth as a
COL. unit toward and away from the palm. Used for all distances. Similar to GOODBYE D, but signals the opposite.

COME

B.

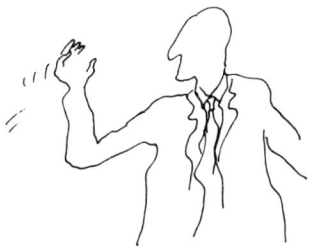

COMMON. Palm is reversed from A. Often used by Colombians to call people at short distances.

COME

C.

COL. Whereas in A the fingers are close together as they move backwards and forwards, here they move one after the other, usually beginning with the smallest. Gesture used much more frequently by women than by men.

COME
    D.

COMMON.   Palm up, index finger moves back and forth.

COME
    E.

COL.   Same as D, but palm is down.

COME
    F.

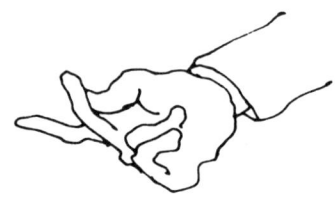

U.S.   Finger Snap. Thumb and second finger are pressed together in tension, finger is released and snapped against palm.

        D, E, and F are used in both cultures by 1) superiors to inferiors (mother-child; patron-waiter; policeman-prisoner, etc.) and 2) among equals in an informal atmosphere (office girls, laboratory technicians, etc.).

COMPLICATION

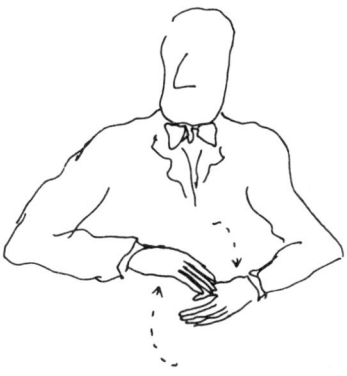

COL.   Hands, fingers loose, rotate over each other.

CROSS
A & B

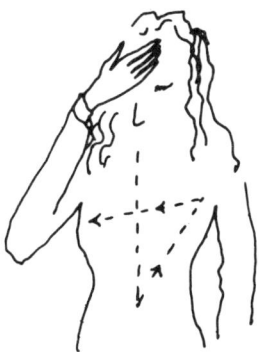

COMMON.   Sign of the Cross. In addition to religious use, may indicate the presence of evil and the need for protection (for example, at times of thunder and lightning). Much more frequent in Colombia.

CROWD

COL. One or both hands form a teardrop shape in front of body; sometimes hands are opened and shut several times, and sometimes hands are shaken.

A lot of people. Bastante, mucha gente.

DANCE
A.

COL. With the index finger extended and pointing downwards, the performer (male) makes circular motions with his hand. Used especially when the male and female are far apart.

DANCE
B.

COMMON.

DELICACY

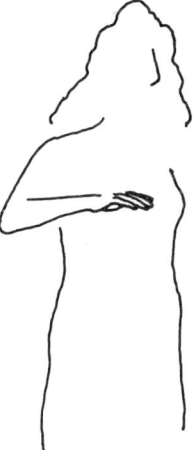

COL.　　Forearm is raised parallel to the ground with hand extended almost touching chest.

It's delicate, fine, etc. Es muy delicado, fino.

DENIAL
A.

COL. Thumb rests between chin and lower lip while fingers, extended, move from side to side. Used frequently in public markets.

We don't have any (with implication of don't bother me anymore).

No hay.

DENIAL
B.

COMMON. Hands moved up and down, palms brushing each other.

I wash my hands of it.

No quiero tenér nada que ver con esto, Yo me lavo las manos en esto.

DENIAL

C.

COL.   Arms are criss-crossed at wrist; palms face away from body. Then hands are moved apart.
See NOTHING (pp. 92, 93).

I don't want anymore. No quiero más.

DIRECTIONS

A.

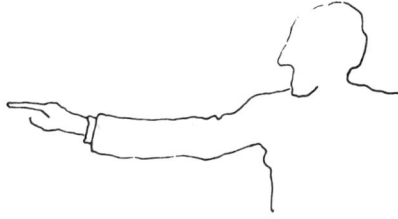

COMMON.   Arm is extended with index finger indicating direction.

DIRECTIONS

B.

COL.   Lips are pursed and then moved in the direction the performer wishes to indicate. Used for nearby people and objects.

DIRECTIONS
C.

COL. With arm bent at elbow and palm up, forearm moves back and forth in the direction indicated.

DIRECTIONS
D.

COMMON. Thumb protruding from fist indicates direction. Whereas in the U.S. this gesture is strong and often rude, in Colombia it is a more acceptable way of indicating direction.

DIRECTIONS
E.

COL.   With arm raised extended hand indicates direction with one or more sharp back and forth movements. Used especially for places at a distance.

DIRECTIONS
F.

COMMON.   Index finger is extended in direction indicated, *Straight ahead. Derecho.*

DIRECTIONS
G.

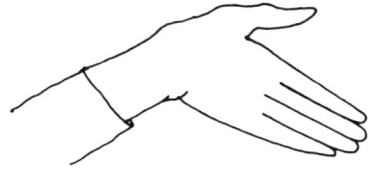

COL.   Hand, with all fingers together, extended in direction indicated. Sometimes both hands are extended.

DISAGREEMENT

A.

COL. A fist is made, as forearm, at a right angle to upper arm, is extended to the front and then moved back and forth several times. An impolite gesture, which is normally a response.

To the contrary. Like hell. Lo contrario.

DISAGREEMENT

B.

COL. Index fingers are pointed at each other, moved back and forth slightly. They may touch.

At odds. De punta.

DISAPPOINTMENT
A.

COL.   Same gesture as DENIAL A.
I've been stood up. I've been stuck. Yo me quedé metido.

DISAPPOINTMENT
B.

COL.   Thumb rests at corner of mouth and palm faces away from the body.

DISAPPROVAL

A.

COMMON. Thumb is extended from fist. Hand often moves up and down several times.

DISAPPROVAL

B.

COMMON. Nose wrinkled and eyes squinted.

DISBELIEF
A.

COL.   Hand is cupped, palm up, about six inches below the chin. Used when a speaker is telling a story or making a statement, and the listener, who performs the gesture, wishes to indicate his disbelief. Is is *not* usually used directly in front of the speaker. The gesture seems to have originated as the description of a goiter, a symbol of stupidity. At first the gesture may have referred to the stupidity or unreliability of the teller: it then could have been used to indicate the shrewdness of the listener who is not so dumb as to believe the tale or claim of the teller.

DISBELIEF
B.

COL.   Index finger moves lightly up and down throat several times. Often accompanied by widening of the lips.

HANDBOOK OF GESTURES

DISBELIEF

C.

COMMON. Lips, held tightly, slowly widen. Sometimes accompanied by a nodding of the head and the sounds *m-hmmmmmm* in English.

DISBELIEF

D.

COMMON. Eye wink. Performer indicates to a second person that a verbal message to or from a third person is not to be believed or is a joke.

DISBELIEF

E.

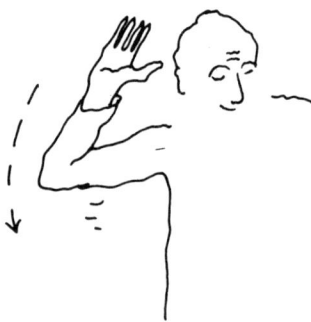

U.S. Head of the performer is turned away from the speaker; one arm is raised in front of the body, hand extended, with palm facing away from the body. Often the hand is then brought down briskly.

DISBELIEF
F.

U.S. Eyes widened eyebrows raised. Corners of mouth drawn. The drawing down of the corners of the mouth often indicates belittlement, disparagement. (*Big deal!*)

DISBELIEF
G.

U.S. With fist closed, thumb points at referent; one eye often half closes. Lips purse or lip corners tighten.

Get him.

**DISBELIEF
H.**

U.S.   Performer makes motions of shoveling from the ground over his shoulder. Usually humorous. Male. Implies that performer does not believe exaggerations or lies of speaker.
Shoveling it. Throwing the bull (the *it* and *bull* refer to cattle manure).
Pura paja.

**DISBELIEF
I.**

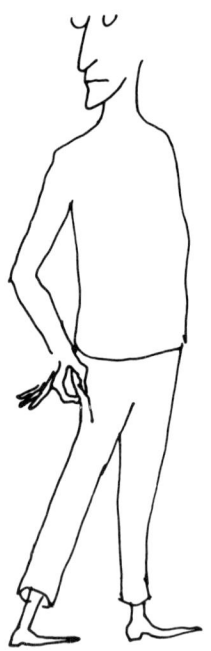

U.S.   Performer lifts pant leg as if wading carefully in deep manure. Male. Humorous. Used in same context as DISBELIEF H.

DISGUST

COMMON. In both Colombia and the United States, the outstretched hand, fingers together, palm down, is placed at right angles to different parts of the body — the chest, the neck, the head. In the United States it is more common for the hand to rest against the neck; in Colombia, the hand frequently rests on top of the head. Reported (1970) as not very common among young adults in U.S.

I've had it up to here. Hasta aquí, Estoy harto.

In both the U.S. and Colombia, spitting is a rude male sign of extreme disgust.

DISINTEREST

COMMON. Shrug of shoulders. Often accompanied by tightening of the lips. When a Colombian child uses this gesture to an older person, it is considered very impolite.
See NERVOUSNESS (p. 92) and MORE OR LESS (p. 91)
I don't care. No me importa.

DRINK
    A   (Thirst)

    COL.   Hand is raised to mouth, thumb extended and pointing at mouth, little finger raised. Hand rocks back and forth in this position.

I'm thirsty. Tengo sed.

DRINK
    B.   (Thirst)

    U.S.   Tongue protrudes over lower lip. Often comic.

DRINK
    C.   (Double Drink)

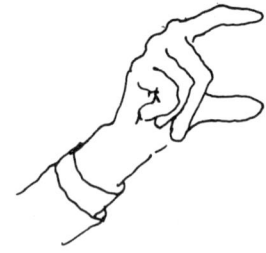

    COMMON.   May indicate the amount desired or a double drink.

DRINK

D.   (Double Drink)

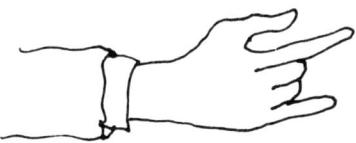

COL.   This gesture should not be confused with INSULTS (Cuckold).

DRUNK

COL.   Usually same as DRINK A. Occasionally hand may twist from side to side instead of moving back and forth.

He's drunk. Esta borracho.

EMPHASIS (Conversational)

In both cultures, speakers emphasize points in conversations with a variety of arm and hand movements. Their nature and frequency vary with the individual. In general, the Colombian has a greater variety than people in the United States and he uses them with a much higher frequency. Below are included a few of the more striking gestures used for special imphasis in conversation.

EMPHASIS
    A.

    COMMON.   Fist strikes palm (or a surface such as a table) once or several times in succession.

EMPHASIS
    B.

    Ambiguous   Fingers of hand are extended as heel of palm strikes forehead.
    COL.   In the U.S., this normally indicates forgetfulness or chagrin. See MEMORY (pp. 86, 87). In Colombia, it can be used as a superlative:

    He's the most . . . El es/esta el más . . .

EMPHASIS
C.

COL.   Hand sweeps upward and outward, with palm facing away from body.

EMPHASIS
D.

Ambiguous Finger of borth hands come to a point and tap chest. Male
COL.   gesture similar to gesture for SELF. SELF A (p. 113) and
           PERFECTION A (p. 95).

ENCOURAGEMENT
A.

COMMON. Hand, palm open, strikes back once or several times lightly.

ENCOURAGEMENT
B.

U.S. Hand, palm open, strikes buttocks once. Common only on sports teams.

See APPROVAL E (p. 21) for another U.S. gesture of encouragement, applause.

ENTHUSIASM

A.

COMMON. A strong hand clasp. More commonly female.

How wonderful!   ¡Qué divino!

ENTHUSIASM

B.

COMMON. Hands raised, fingers outstretched, mouth often open. Usually female and often accompanied by intake of breath.

See Gestures of APPROVAL (pp. 19-21) for other gestures that indicate ENTHUSIASM.

EXCITEMENT
A.

COMMON. Hands are held in front of body, palms facing each other about twelve inches apart. Hands are then clasped. Much more common in Colombia. Female.

EXCITEMENT
B.

COMMON. Open hand covers mouth. Often used in context of impending danger.

FAT

COMMON.   Cheeks are filled with air as hands indicate extent of waist.

FAUX PAS
A.

COMMON.   Index finger is moved across throat.

FAUX PAS
B.

COMMON. Thumb and index finger form pistol shape, as performer imitates the act of shooting himself in the temple.
Thumb may be sent or erect.

I put my foot in it.   Meté la pata.

FAUX PAS
C.   (Trouble)

COMMON. Eyebrows are raised and pupils focused upward. Melodramatic
See REGRETS (pp. 100-102) for additional gestures of chagrin and FAUX PAS.

HANDBOOK OF GESTURES 53

FAVOR
   A.

COL.   Hand brushes shoulder lightly, imitating action of brushing.

Apple Polishing. Cepillar.

FAVOR
   B.

U.S.   Hand, held in fist, makes twisting motion around tip of nose.

Brown-Nosing. Cepillar.

54   HANDBOOK OF GESTURES

FEMALE

COMMON. Hands shape, exaggeratedly, the outline of an attractive female figure.

FIGHT

COL. Fist is held out to the side at about chin level, and moved back and forth several times.

FLIRTATION (Wink)

COMMON. Eye Wink. While a slow wink is often flirtatious and an invitation to intimacy, a quick wink, particularly in the U.S., may signal only conviviality, a friendliness without the connotation of intimacy.

FOLLOWING

COMMON. Thumb extended from hand points to the rear. Used particularly by vehicle drivers to indicate that another vehicle is coming.

FOOD
A.

COL.   Cupped fingers of one hand move back and forth in front of open mouth. Women often move one finger after another.

FOOD
B.

COMMON.   One hand is rubbed back and forth across the stomach. Often comic.

HANDBOOK OF GESTURES 57

FOOD
C.

COL.   Both fists are held against stomach as mouth is opened. Rural.

FOOD A, B, C :   *I'm hungry. I want to eat.*
Tengo hambre. Quiero comér.

FRIENDSHIP

U.S.   Middle finger is crossed over nail of index finger.
See LUCK A.

They, we, are close friends.   Son, somos, íntimos amigos.

FRUSTRATION

COMMON. Fist bangs slowly and repeatedly on table. Lips usually tightened.

FULL (of food)

COMMON. One hand pats stomach gently.

GO

A.   (Traffic Direction)

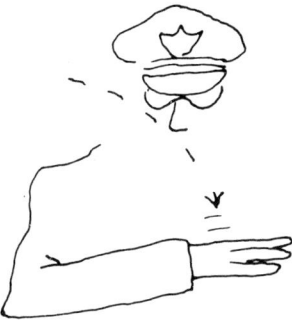

COL.   With palm facing in direction traffic is to go, hand is moved to a position in front of the body, parallel to ground, and held there.

GO

B.   (Traffic Direction)

COL.   Policeman places his body parallel to the direction in which he wants traffic to go.

GO

C.   (Traffic Direction)

COMMON.   With palm facing in direction traffic is to go, hand is held up at head level or slightly above head level, and waved back and forth several times.

GOAD

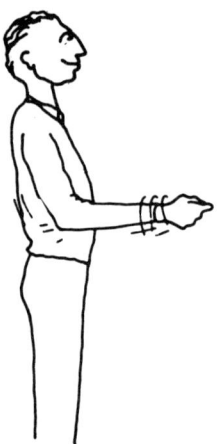

COL.   Hand held in fist, makes a twisting thrust. Forearm extended and parallel to the ground.

GOODBYE

A.

COMMON. Colombians, men and women, shake hands at the beginning and end of meeting much more frequently than people in the United States. The Colombian handshake is used even after long acquaintance and its omission can be a sign of discourtesy. Often during a prolonged farewell, after hands have been shaken once, and then the conversation resumed, it is common for the handshake to be repeated. For people in the United States, the handshake seems formal, a mark of initial encounter and special occasions. The Colombian handshake is likely to last longer the the U.S. one.

GOODBYE

B.

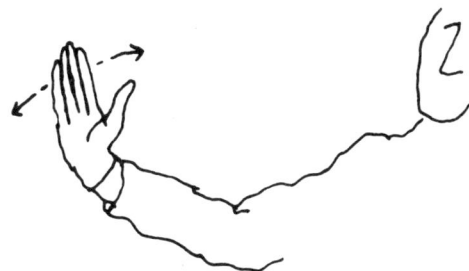

COL. Hand moves more slowly and fingers are closer together than in the U.S. goodbye wave. See GOODBYE C.
Position of hand may vary from in front of body to near ear, but usually it is at face level.

**GOODBYE
C.**

U.S. Fingers are spread apart. Hand waves more rapidly than in GOODBYE B. At times, whole arm moves vigorously.

**GOODBYE
D.**

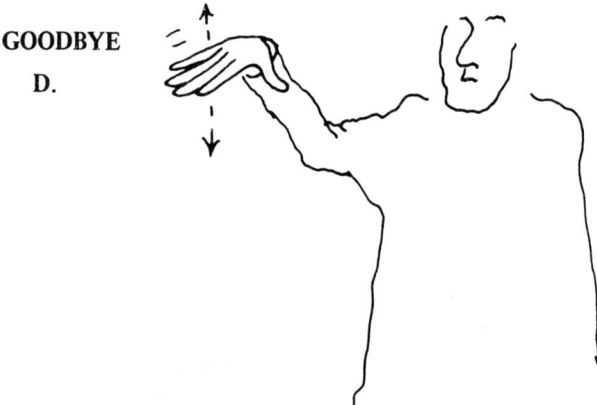

Ambiguous Hand is moved up and down. Fingers are apart.
U.S.

See COME A (p. 27) for a similar Colombian gesture with a different meaning.

GOODBYE

E.

COMMON. The salute, used in same context as *Hello* salute. See GREETINGS I (p. 69).

GOODBYE

F.

COMMON.

GOODBYE

G.

COMMON. Although GOODBYES F & G may be intimate gestures in both cultures, as with the wink, individuals may adopt them for casual use.

GOSSIP

COL.   Tongue is extended and index finger, bent, touches it.

GRAFT

COL.   One hand, fingers extended, makes a sawing motion on the side of the other hand.

Saw. Serrucho.

GREETINGS
A.

COMMON. See GOODBYE A (p. 61).

GREETINGS
B.

COL. Hand, palm facing body, moves sharply from a point not far from temple out to the side and up. An informal greeting which can precede a handshake. Observed particularly in the province of Boyaca: not common in the large cities.

GREETINGS
C.

COL. Index and second fingers are extended from hand and held together tightly, pointing upwards. A casual greeting.

GREETINGS
D.

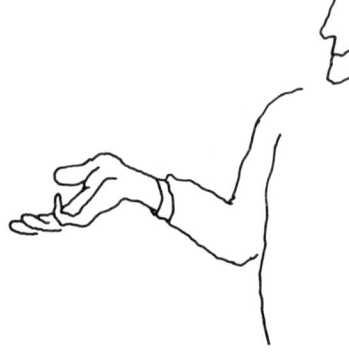

COL.   One hand, palm up, is held out to the side at waist level or slightly above. Used normally when the greeters are at some distance from each other. When the greeters are within speaking distance, the gesture is very frequently accompanied by *Qué hubo,* (Hi, How are you). Male gesture primarily. Note similarity to SEXUAL E (p. 116).

GREETINGS
E.

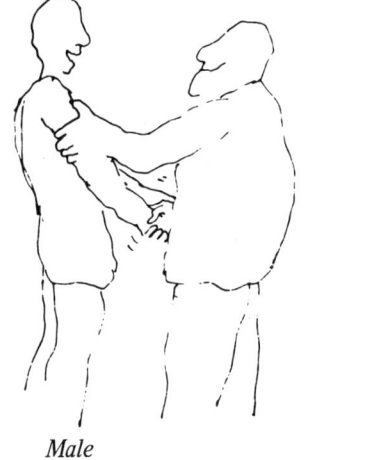

Male   *Female*

COL.   The grasping of each other's arms is an affectionate, enthusiastic greeting used occasionally by men and women. The male will grasp the forearm or upper arm of another male; the second male will grasp the upper arm or the shoulder of the first. Often, instead of a grasp, a patting motion will be used. Women usually grasp each other's forearms. This greeting among women observed especially in the cities.

GREETINGS
F.

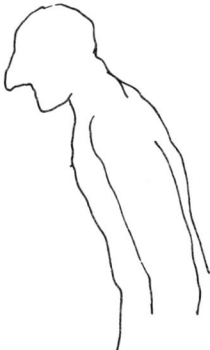

COL.   The forward bow, using either the head alone or the whole upper part of the body, while standing or walking, is a greeting of minimum courtesy to acquaintances, usually male. It is polite, but not warm, and usually indicates that a conversation will not take place at that time. On a campus of a Colombian university, for example, a professor would normally greet his fellows teachers, the clergy, and university officials (many of whom he encounters several times a day) in this way. The United States male, who bows very infrequently—usually to mock formality, will do so with the upper part of his body, rather than his head alone.

GREETINGS
G.

COL.   Hat is tipped by grasping crown with fingers and either raising the hat a bit or removing it completely. At the same time head and upper part of body move forward. Hats can be tipped to both men and women.

GREETINGS
H.

U.S.   Hat is tipped by grasping brim and raising it slightly or simply by touching brim with fingers. Normally hats are tipped only to women.

In Colombia, hats are worn primarily by rural, highland families (the whole family), though when the families migrate to the cities, usually only the male retains his hat. City people, especially younger ones, tend not to wear hats. Since the weather is mild and there are no significant seasonal changers, hat wearing does not vary according to the time of year, as it does in the U.S. In both Colombia and the United States men remove their hats when entering homes, offices and elevators. In Colombia it is also common, particularly on country roads, for men to raise their hats when passing a religious shrine or a church.

GREETINGS

I.

COMMON.   Salute. In both Colombia and the United States the salute, when not used in military contexts, is often a humorous gesture for *hello*.

GREETINGS

J.

COMMON.   Eyebrows raised and lowered quickly, often accompanied by a nod or a smile. A casual greeting, usually used by greeters separated by some distance (as across a crowded room).
A concomitant of the Colombian greeting gestures is the custom of standing up whenever a newcomer, male or female, enters the room. A seated female may or may not rise, a male always. The more formal the occasion, the more likelihood of everyone rising. At times, standing may be omitted if the newcomer insists or if there are so many in the room that it is unfeasible. Standing may be repeated at leave-taking, also.
In general, the more noticeable gestures of greeting and leave-taking (handshaking, rising, etc.) are not used as frequently or consistently by people in the United States as by Colombians, and it should be noted that the omission of such movements by Americans should not be interpreted as a discourtesy (it is often, in fact, an indication of the opposite—informality and ease).

HANDBOOK OF GESTURES

HEIGHT

A.

COL. This is used *only* for indicating the height of *human beings*.

HEIGHT

B.

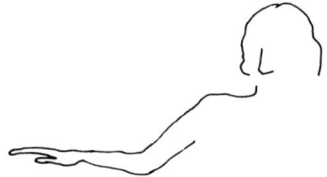

Ambiguous. In the United States this is used for both human beings and animals. In most of Colombia, with the exception of some parts of the north coast, it is used *only* for *animals*.

HITCHHIKING

U.S. Hand with thumb extended in the direction the performer wishes to go can remain stationary or it can move back and forth. Colombians would use *Stop* gesture (See STOP pp. 130-131). for requesting a vehicle to stop, although hitchhiking is not as common as in the U.S.

HOT

A.

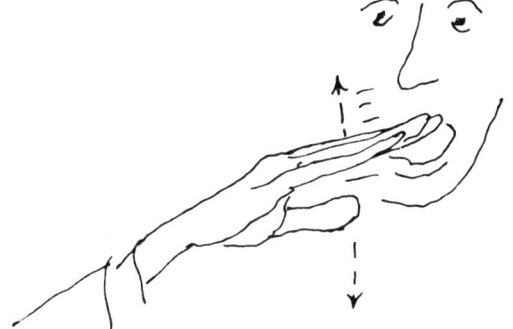

COMMON. Hand, parallel to the ground, moves up and down in front of open mouth. Rare in Colombia. Refers to food which is very warm or spicy.

It's hot. Está caliente (hot). *Está picante* (spicy).

HOT

B.

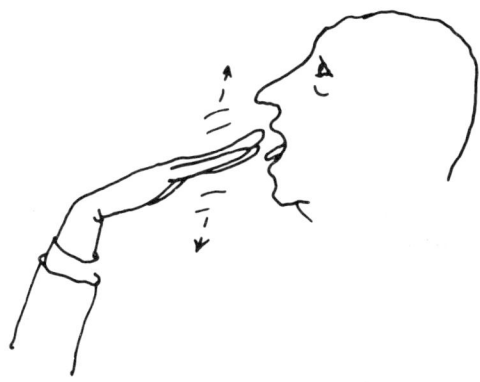

U.S. With palm facing mouth, fingers move up and down. Refers to food, as in HOT A.

HOT

C.

U.S. One hand, fingers extended, palm facing forehead, moves across forehead, and then shakes once, as if throwing away perspiration. Refers to weather or personal discomfort.

I'm hot. Tengo calór. It's hot. Hace calór.

IMPATIENCE
A.

COL. One hand is slapped lightly against thigh and remains there a moment. Often indicates imminent castigation for a child when used by a parent or elder.

IMPATIENCE
B.

COMMON. One foot is tapped several times on the ground. Hands may be placed on hips or folded across chest.

IMPATIENCE
C.

U.S.   Fingers drum surface rhythmically usually beginning with little finger and moving to thumb. Also may indicate boredom.

IMPRISONMENT
A.

COL.   One hand grasps wrist of other hand.

IMPRISONMENT
B.

COL.   One hand grasps throat.

IMPRISONMENT A & B indicate the possibility or actuality of imprisonment.

INSANITY

A.

COMMON. Index finger, extended from a fist, points toward side of head as finger makes a circular motion.

INSANITY

B.

COMMON. Index finger is tapped lightly against temple.
See INTELLIGENCE (p. 78)

Crazy. Loco, chiflado.

INSULTS

A.

COMMON. Used by children and, jokingly, by adults.

INSULTS

B.

COMMON. Fingers of both hands move backwards and forwards; used by children.

INSULTS
C.

COMMON. Fingers move from side to side. Used particularly by children in the U.S., but by adults in Colombia.

INSULTS
D.

COL. Fingers move from side to side.

INSULTS

E.

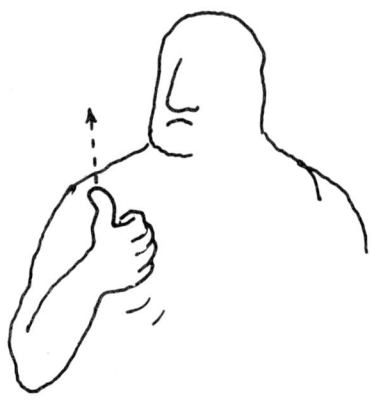

U.S. Thumb is extended from fist; hand moves up and down several times. Considered a vulgar gesture. Male.

See SEXUAL A, B, C, D, E (pp. 114-116) for other strong male insults.

INTELLIGENCE

COMMON. Index finger is tapped lightly against temple, or forehead; at times it is simply placed at the temples.

HANDBOOK OF GESTURES 79

KISS

A. (Request for)

COMMON. Tongue protrudes slightly between lips and moves slowly along width of lips. Primarily a masculine gesture, often used by adolescents.

Compare ANTICIPATIONS B (p. 18), and SEXUAL H (p. 117).

KISS

B.

COL. Lips kiss palm. Then hand is extended. Usually used when performer and referent are some distance from each other.

KISS

C.

COMMON. Lips kiss tips of extended fingers. Then hand is extended.

A kiss may also be signalled by puckering the lips and imitating the sound of the kiss, while raising the head and moving the chin slightly forward.

LEAVE
A.

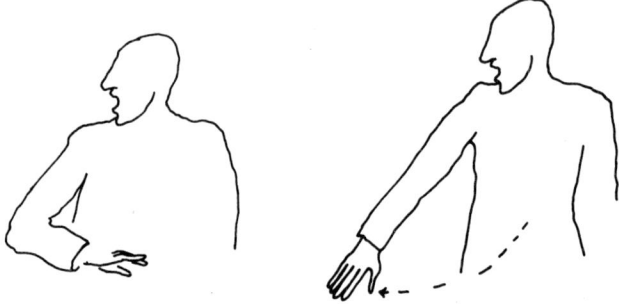

COL.   Forearm is horizontal to waist. Fingers held together and extended, palm facing away from body. Hand moves out to the side sharply.

LEAVE
B.

U.S.   Hand with thumb extended moves back and forth indicating the direction of the desired departure. Male. Impolite.

Out! Afuera!

LEAVE
C.

COMMON.   Index finger indicates direction of the desired movement.

LEAVE
D.

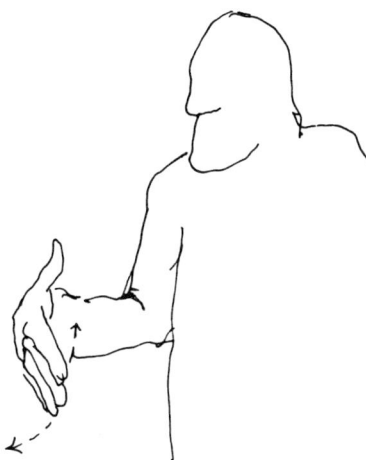

COL. With palm facing body, hand moves back and forth in front of body in short, sharp movements.

LEAVE
E.

COMMON. A kicking motion, as if performer were kicking a ball. Male. Rude. Often comic.

LUCK

A.

COMMON. Middle finger is crossed over index finger. In Colombia, this gesture frequently indicates the performer's desire to avoid an unwelcome person or event. In the U.S., in addition to the general meaning of "May bad luck be avoided", it may be used by the speaker while he is lying (presumably to ward off the evil that the lying might cause him).

LUCK

B.

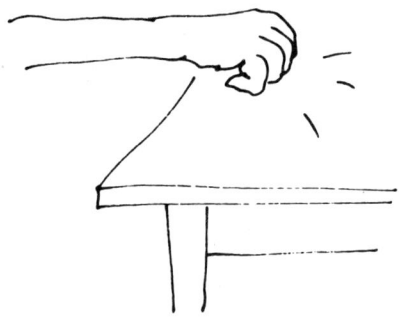

COMMON. Performer raps his knockles on a piece of wood — indicates that 1) someone has had good luck or that 2) he hopes good luck will continue.

Knock on wood. Diós no lo permita.

LUCK

C.   (Hope for marriage)

COL.   A girl, upon seeing three priests or three negroes, will scratch her knee or knot her head-scarf. This is supposed to bring her luck in finding a husband soon. This gesture may be taken as an insult by the groups of three. Rural.

LUCK

D.   (the lizard charm)

COL.   Index and little fingers are extended from fist. Hand then rotates from side to side several times. To counteract possible effect of the utterance of the taboo word *culebra* (*snake*) the performer says *lagarto* (*lizard*) and makes this gesture.

Compare SEXUAL R (p. 121).

MARRIAGE
A.

COMMON. Index finger taps ring finger. In Colombia, wedding rings are worn on the right hand after marriage and it is common for an unmarried girl to wear a simple goldband on her left hand before marriage. In the United States, the wedding ring is worn on the left hand. In both Colombia and the United States, the third finger is the ring finger.

MARRIAGE
B.

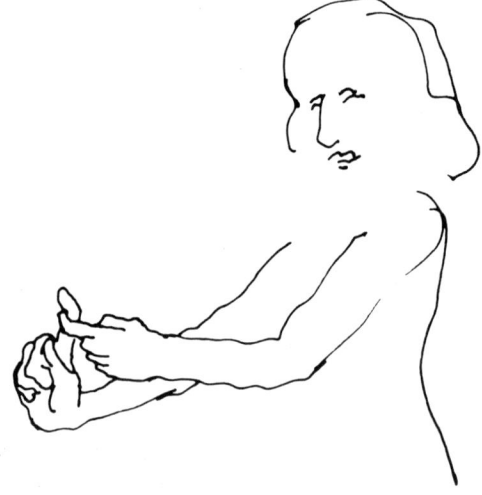

COL. Index fingers are linked.

MASCULINITY

COL.   Fist, with thumb resting on side of index finger, moves up and down sharply several times.

Macho (He-Man)

STRENGTH B (p. 133) is also used as a gesture of Masculinity in both cultures.

MEMORY
A.   (Forgetting)

COMMON.   Finger Snap. Thumb and second finger are pressed together in tension; finger is released and snapped against palm.

MEMORY
B.   (Remembering)

COMMON.   Same as MEMORY A

MEMORY
C. (Forgetting–Remembering)

COMMON. One hand, fingers extended, is placed on the forehead, or side of face or back of head. Forgetting gestures may be accompanied by

I forgot it. Se me olvidó.

MEMORY
D. (Remembering)

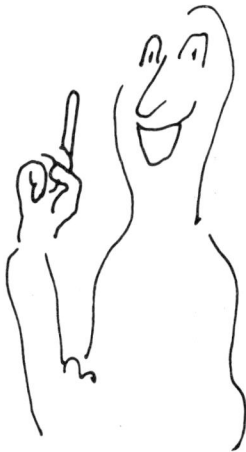

U.S. Index finger extended upward from fist and held at shoulder level. Eyebrows raised, often accompanied by *Aha*. Melodramatic.

MONEY
A.

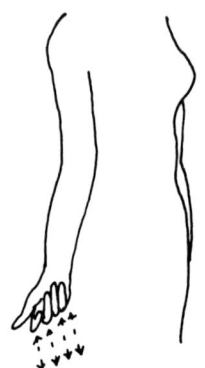

COL.   Palm faces the person being addressed. Fingers, as a unit, or one after the other, move backwards and forwards.

MONEY
B.

COL.   Forearm held up and fingers point down as they move, as a unit, or one at a time, backwards and forwards.

MONEY
C.

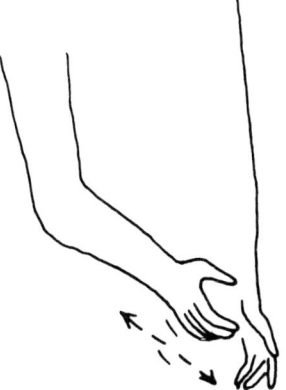

COL.   Fingers of one hand scrape the palm of the other hand lightly.

MONEY
D. (Pay me)

U.S.   Palm facing upward, is extended in front of body. This gesture is also common as the gesture for *give it to me*, referring to any object the speaker wants. SEE REQUESTS (pp. 104, 105).

90   HANDBOOK OF GESTURES

MONEY

E.

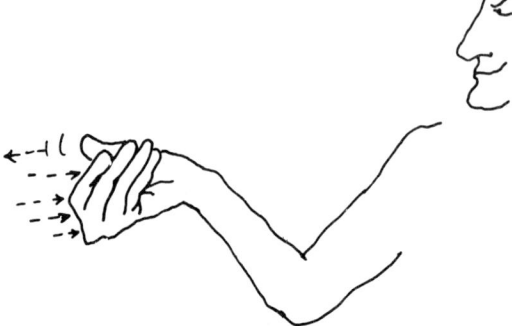

U.S.   Fingers and thumb of the same hand rub against each other. Occasionally both hands are used.

MONEY

F.   (No)

COMMON. Insides of pockets are pulled out. Male. Not as common in Colombia as in U.S.

MONEY GESTURES A, B, C, and E are also used for *I don't have any money* (*no tengo plata*), in which case they might be accompanied by verbal or gestural negation.

MORE OR LESS
A.

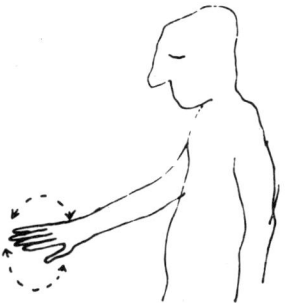

COMMON.   Palm, facing downward, remains parallel with floor, as hand rocks slightly from side to side. *Más o menos* (*more or less, so-so*).

SEE SEXUAL O (p. 120).

MORE OR LESS
B.

COMMON.   Head moves slowly from one side to the other. Often indicates an unenthusiastic reaction.

NERVOUSNESS

COMMON. Twiddling the thumbs. Fingers are interlocked, while thumbs are rotated around each other.

See BOREDOM (p. 25) and THOUGHT (pp. 139-142) for other gestures indicating nervousness.

NO INFORMATION
A.

COL. Hands, palms facing away from body, are held up in front of body and then moved slightly to the sides. A slight pursing of the lips usually accompanies this gesture.

NO INFORMATION
B.

COL. One hand is held up in front or out to the side of body, palm facing away from body. Often accompanied by tightening of mouth and head tilt. Often used in contexts where the performer wishes to indicate that he can add no more to what has been said, or that the subject is beyond him.

NO INFORMATION
C.

COMMON.   Shoulders are raised slightly as lips are pursed.

NO INFORMATION
D.

COL.   Hands move out to the sides.

NO INFORMATION
E.

U.S.   Head Scratching.

These gestures are usually responses to *What happened? – Que pasó?*, but are also frequently used to indicate *"We can't do anything about it – Que podemos hacér?"*

OATH
A.

COL. Nail of thumb is kissed; index finger rests against the thumb, while the other fingers are raised. In the second stage of the gesture, hand moves away from mouth quickly, as thumb and index finger separate. At times, the kiss is not made, and the hand, in the same position as in stage (1), is held out in front of the body. Often accompanied by the words *Por esta, la crúz* (*by this, the cross*). — *Te lo juro* (*I swear it*).

OATH
B.

COMMON. Right hand is raised to shoulder — head level or slightly above.

I swear it! Lo juro!

PERFECTION
A.

COL.   Thumb and index finger in front of the body, above the waist, from a circle parallel to the ground. Hand is sometimes moved up and down.

See SEXUAL M (p. 119) for a similar gesture.

PERFECTION
B.

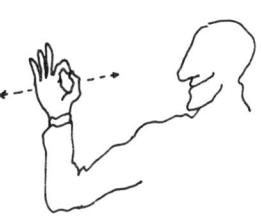

COMMON.   With hand at eye level in front of body, thumb and index finger form a circle. Hand sometimes moves back and forth slightly. Reported as recent in Colombia.

PHOTOGRAPH

COMMON.   Hands make motions of holding a camera up to the eyes and snapping a picture. May mean photograph or taking a picture.

PRIDE
A.

U.S.   Thumbs are hooked under the armpits as palms face each other. Comic. This gesture, recognized by some Colombians, is almost never used in Colombia.

PRIDE
B.

U.S.   Performer blows upon finger nails of one hand, and then rubs nails on the front of his body. Comic.

HANDBOOK OF GESTURES

PRIDE

C.

U.S.   Performer pats himself on top of shoulder with one hand.

PROXIMITY and TOUCHING

Colombians stand and sit closer to each other than do people in the U.S. Whereas in the U.S. the normal social distance between people falls between 18 and 36 inches, it is often between 12 and 18 inches in Colombia. This difference seems reflected in behavior in public places: waiting lines are more compact; busses can be loaded beyond imaginable capacity, and all conversations look intimate to someone from the U.S.

Colombians also seem to touch each other more frequently in social contexts (not intimate) than do people in the U.S.. In conversation, the Colombian will often make a gesture of reaching out to his companion; he will touch him on the arm or shoulder. Colombian males, as well as females, will stroll arm in arm. And in crowded places in Colombia where one unavoidably bumps or jostles against a neighbor, the contact is not treated as exceptional: it is common to omit the equivalent of the U.S. expression "Sorry", "Excuse me", etc., which people in the U.S. use so frequently when body contact is made accidentally.

PUNISHMENT
A.

COL.   Performer pulls nose.

PUNISHMENT
B.

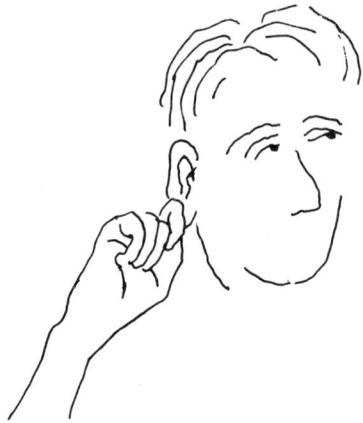

COL.   Performer pulls ear. Pulling of the nose or ear anticipates punishment of either referent or performer. For example, a little boy might pull his ear as he foresees punishment by a parent; one man might pull his nose to indicate that a second man will be scolded by his wife.

QUICKLY

U.S.   Finger snap.

RECOGNITION

COL.   One eye, looking in direction of the referent, closes slowly.

Creo que lo conozco. I think I know him.

REGRET   (Chagrin)
A.

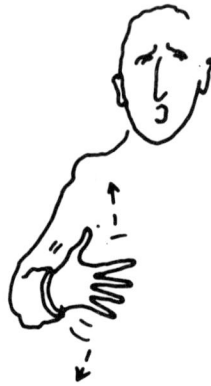

COL.   Palm (or palms) faces body as hand is held in front of the body. Fingers are held loosely, as hand is shaken up and down violently.

REGRET

B.

COL.   As in REGRET A, hand is shaken in front of body. Thumb and middle finger are then pressed together. The arm is snapped violently, like a whip, and index finger slaps sharply and loudly against middle finger.

REGRET
   C.

   COMMON.   Hand (or both hands) is raised to side of head, palm inward resting on cheek or side of head.

   What have I done? Ay, qúe he hecho!

REGRET
   D.

   COL.   Tongue protrudes over upper lip. Often accompanied by a finger flap as in REGRET B.

REGRET

    E.

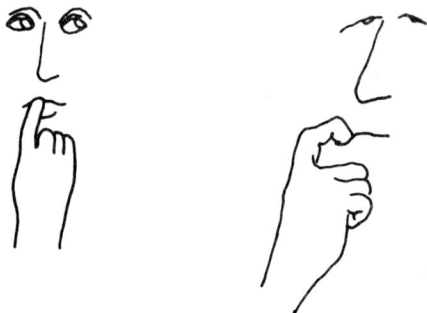

COMMON.   One or more fingers are inserted between the lips or teeth.

REGRET

    F.

COMMON.   Hand is clapped over mouth quickly.

See FAUX PAS (pp. 51, 52) for more dramatic gestures of REGRET.

REPETITION
A.

COL. Circling motion with index finger.
May mean *come back again* (*no pierda el camino*); *another one* (*otro*), etc.

See RESTAURANT (p. 109) and WHAT? (p. 149).

REPETITION
B.

COL. Performer grasps part of his clothing (sweater, skirt, jacket) and, bunching it, pulls it a bit forward or to the side. Performer thus indicates that which he is hearing is repetitious.

Muñeca. Doll.

REQUESTS
A.

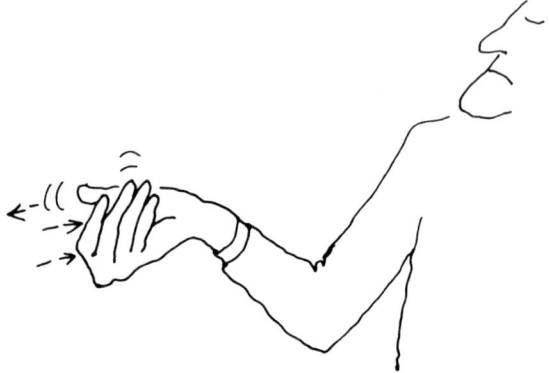

COMMON.   Hand extended with palm up. Most common gesture for *Give it to me (damelo)*.

REQUESTS
B.

COMMON.   Fingers and thumb of one or both hands rub.

REQUESTS
C.

COL.   To ask for the ball during a game (as in volleyball), the Colombian often claps his hands. Particularly noticeable among females.

REQUESTS
D.

COMMON.   Used specifically for requesting a ball during a game.

See RESTAURANT (pp. 106-110) and COME (pp. 27, 28) for more REQUESTS.

RESTAURANT GESTURES

    A.   (waiter)

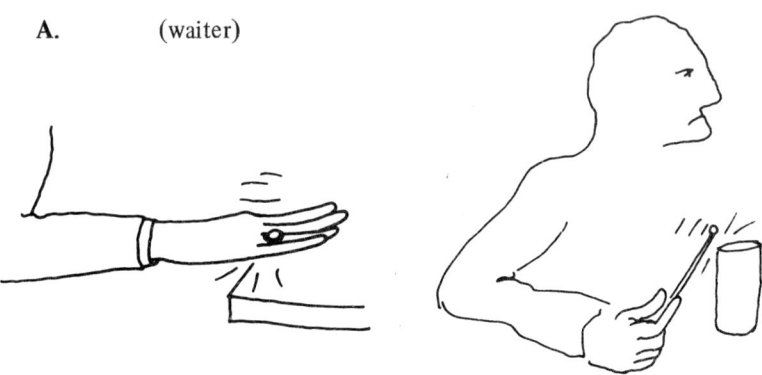

    COL.   The top of the table is tapped sharply with the patron's ring, with a glass, etc.; any object on the table (a glass or cup) may be tapped by another object, such as a spoon.
Thus, sharp sounds are made to get the waiter's attention.

RESTAURANT

    B.   (waiter)

    COL.   Hands are clapped sharply.

RESTAURANT

C.   (waiter)

U.S.   People in the U.S. commonly use facial and head movements to attract the attention of a waiter. The patron "catches the waiter's eye" (i.e. he tries to look at him directly), or raises his eyebrows or stretches his neck or turns his head in the direction the waiter might be expected to appear from.

Colombians also call a waiter by the use of a hissing sound, short and sharp (*sss*).

And we should note that WAITER A & B and the hissing sound are normal Colombian means of getting attention, not as impolite as they appear to people in the U.S.

In the U.S., there is no guaranteed means of getting a waiter's attention; the Colombian gestures (WAITER A & B) and the hissing sound would all be considered rude in U.S. restaurants. The person in the U.S. varies his methods considerably; at times he raises his hand; if the waiter is near, he may call out "*Waiter*" or "*Miss*" (*mesero, señorita*); he may clear his throat; but most frequently he uses eye, face and head movements.

RESTAURANT
D.   (Request for table)

For one person, index finger is raised; for two people index and middle finger; for three people, index, middle and ring fingers; for four people, index, middle, ring, and small fingers; for five people, all fingers.

RESTAURANT
E.   (Request for check)

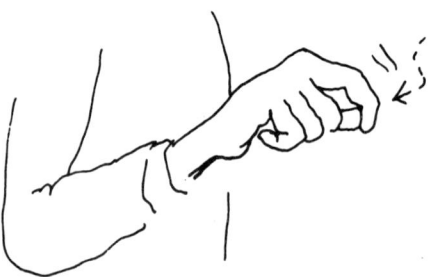

COMMON.   Patron makes motion of writing, in the air.

RESTAURANT
F.   (Request for check)

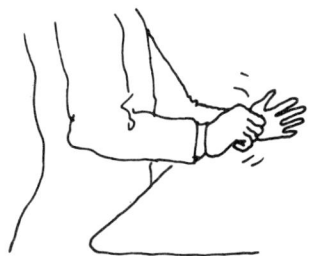

COMMON.   Patron makes motion of writing on his palm.

RESTAURANT
G.   (Request for check)

Ambiguous COL.   Circling motion made with index finger indicating items to be paid for (such as bottles of beer) or people whose checks are to be paid for.

See RESTAURANT H (p. 110).

RESTAURANT

H.   (Request for another round)

Ambiguous   Index finger points down as in RESTAURANT G above.
U.S.

Another round of drinks. Otra vuelta/otra ronda.

RESTAURANT

I.   (Request for another round)

U.S.   Index finger points up as circling motion is made.

See COME (pp. 27, 28) for other requests that might be used in restaurants.

RETRIBUTION (Ironic Applause)

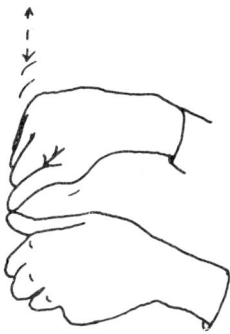

COL.   Thumbs are extended from fists of both hands. One hand is held above other; edge of thumbnail of upper hand touches thumbnail of lower hand. Upper hand may move up and down several times. This is an *I-told-you-so* gesture. Used as silent applause in other countries (Panama, for example), it was observed as non-ironic applause only once in Colombia.

REVENGE

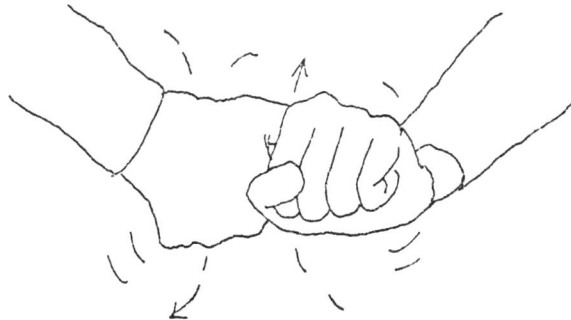

COMMON.   Fists twist and slowly pull away from each other. Used more by children in Colombia. FIGHT gesture is also used in Colombia for revenge.

REVIEW

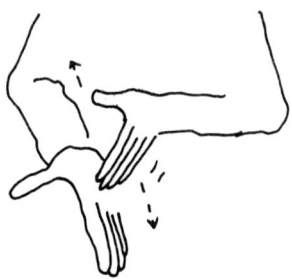

COL.   Fingers of one hand brush palm of the other several times. Used to describe a review (repaso) of written material — books, notes, etc.

SAINTLINESS

COMMON.   Hands are held palm to palm as in prayer. Sometimes comic.

HANDBOOK OF GESTURES   113

SELF (Me)
A.

U.S.   Index finger points at chest.

SELF

B.

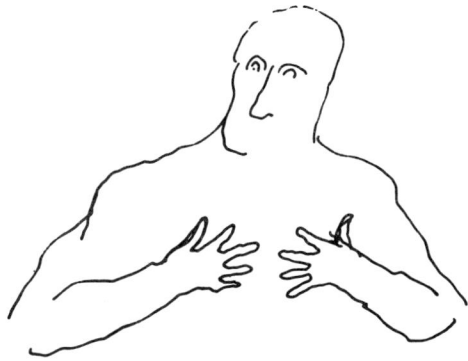

COMMON.   One or both hands, fingers outstretched and spread may rest on chest.

Note:

Not only is there a great variety of pronominal gestures (involving eye, lip, and head movements, for example), but there are also a good many kinesic movements that accompany the use of pronouns. For detail, see Ray L. Birdwhistell, "Communication Without Words" and *Kinesics in Context.* –

114 HANDBOOK OF GESTURES

SEXUAL GESTURES

SEXUAL
  A.   (Phallic)

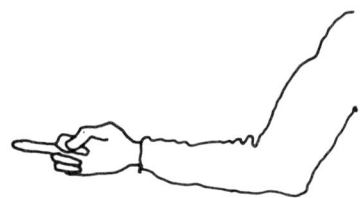

COMMON. Index finger, ring finger and little finger are curled back towards palm; middle finger is extended and pointed towards referent.

SEXUAL
  B.   (Phallic)

COMMON. One hand grasps bicep muscle of opposite arm while the arm, its hand in a fist, is raised and lowered several times. The fist may be shaken as well.

SEXUAL C.

(Phallic)

COL.   Index finger of right hand extended while other fingers remain in a fist; then this fist is slapped firmly into palm of left hand, extended index finger going between thumb and index finger of left hand.

SEXUAL D.

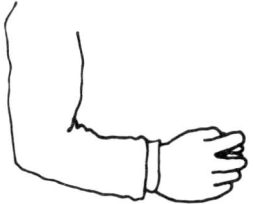

COL.   Thumb placed between index finger and middle finger of same hand as hand makes a fist. Tip of thumb protrudes slightly between fingers. This gesture is used by adults in the U.S. in a game in which they tease young children saying: *"I've got your nose."*

Idiomatic expressions which describe SEXUAL A, B, C, D are: *la pistola* in Colombia and *to give the finger* in the U.S.

116   HANDBOOK OF GESTURES

SEXUAL

E.

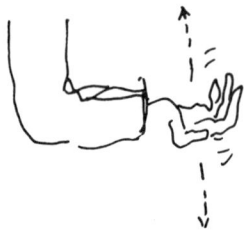

COL.   Cupped hand, palm up, is held in front of chest and moved up and down, in the space of about six inches. Commonly called *huevón* (lit., *large egg*; testicle) in Colombia.

Sexual gestures are strong insults unless they are used jocularly among friends. These gestures are used almost exclusively by and among males. SEXUAL E is a particularly common strong male insult in Colombia.

SEXUAL

F.

COMMON.   Index finger is inserted in loose fist of other hand and finger is moved back and forth several times.

SEXUAL

G.   (Intercourse)

COMMON.   Performer scratches palm of referent with index or middle finger as they shake hands. Used primarily by adolescents.

A proposition.   Una proposición.

HANDBOOK OF GESTURES 117

SEXUAL

H. (Intercourse)

COL. Tongue protrudes slowly between lips. Used most frequently as an invitation to a prostitute.

Compare ANTICIPATION B (p. 18).

SEXUAL

I. (Intercourse)

COL. With fists clenched and forearms extended in front of body just below waist level, arms are jerked back as hips thrust forward.

118   HANDBOOK OF GESTURES

SEXUAL

J.   (Prostitute)

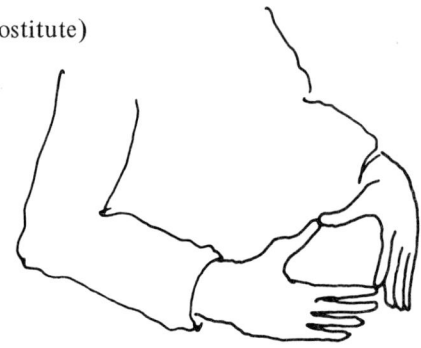

COL.   Index fingers and thumbs of both hands are joined together to form a diamond shape.

SEXUAL

K.   (Prostitute)

COL.   One hand, fingers extended and palm down, moves back and forth in front of body.

SEXUAL

L. (Homosexual)

COMMON. Forearm raised; hand extended but limp with fingers slightly bent; palm facing away from body. Hand may be held in this position momentarily or it may be moved forward. Head usually inclined slightly to one side. Accompanied by smile.

SEXUAL

M.

COL. Thumb and index finger form circle; other fingers are curled back slightly. Circle is made parallel to ground as hand is held near waist. May also occur as a description of vagina.
Compare with PERFECTION (p. 95).

SEXUAL

    N.   (Homosexual)

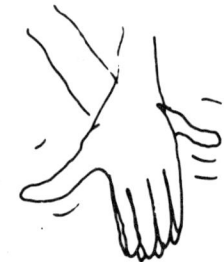

    COL.   One hand rests on top of the other as thumbs flap like the wings of a bird. This gesture is called *Pajaro (Bird)*.

SEXUAL

    O.   (Homosexual)

    COL.   Same gesture as MORE OR LESS A (p. 91).

HANDBOOK OF GESTURES 121

SEXUAL
P.   (Lesbian)

COL.   Hands are held palm to palm and rubbed together lightly. Compare with ANTICIPATION A (p. 17).

SEXUAL
Q.   (Cuckold)

COL.   Index fingers are held along the temples to form horns. Gesture is called *Cuernos (Horns)*; *Cabron* (lit. *big goat*).

SEXUAL
R.   (Cuckold)

COL.   Index or little fingers extended from fist form horns. See SEXUAL Q.

SEXUAL

    S.   (Masturbation)

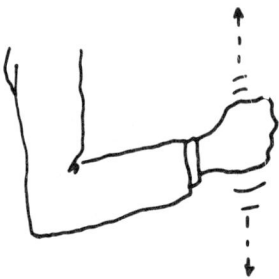

COMMON. Loosely clenched fist is moved up and down in front of body.

SEXUAL

    T.   (Breasts)

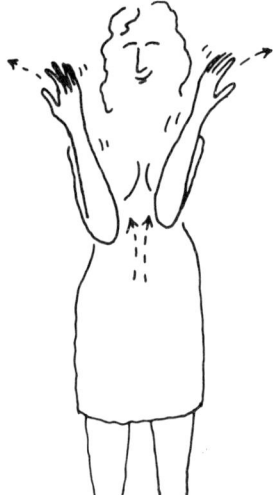

COL.   Performer pretends to throw long, pendulous breasts backwards over shoulders. Indicates exceptionally large breasts.
Both cultures use a variety of hand motions which describe breasts by imitative tracing of the breast form.

SHAME

U.S. Index finger extended from fist rubs over other extended index finger several times. A teasing gesture used by children.

Shame on you! (*Que Vergüenza!*)

See WARNING E (p. 149) which can also indicate SHAME.

SILENCE

A.

COMMON. Index finger extended, touches lips. Often accompanied by pursed lips, and a shushing sound, *SH*, in English.

SILENCE

B.

COMMON. Thumb extended moves from one corner of closed lips to other corner. May mean *silence* (*silencio*) or *to keep a secret* (*guardar un secreto*). *Zip your lip.*

SIT

COMMON. Hand, palm up, fingers extended, is moved toward place indicated for seating. See GREETINGS G (p. 67) for U.S. and COL. difference in bowing.

Won't you sit down please? Siéntese (por favór).

SLEEP
A.

COMMON.   Fingers extended, tap open mouth lightly, several times covering a yawn (*bostezo*).
Considered impolite in formal social contexts.

SLEEP
B.

COMMON.   Hands, fingers extended, are put palm to palm, as in praying; then hands are placed along one cheek, as head is bent to one side. Eyes are often closed at the same time. Female gesture. Often used to signal that someone is sleeping.

126   HANDBOOK OF GESTURES

SLOW DOWN (Traffic)

U.S.   Arms held out to sides, hands extended, fingers together, palms down. Hands move up and down, slowly or rapidly. Body often stooped.

A recent gesture used by policemen on superhighways as a signal to reduce speed.

For other gestures to signal vehicles, See STOP (pp. 130, 131) and GO (pp. 59, 60).

SMALL

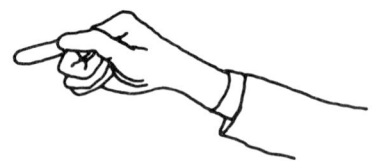

COL.   Index finger is extended from a fist and thumb rests against side of first joint of extended finger.

SMELL (Bad)
A.

COMMON. Nostrils are held shut briefly with thumb and index finger. *Phew. Púf.*

SMELL
B.

COL. Index finger moves up and down between upper lip and nose. Colombians may also fan the air in front of their noses and males occassionally spit in the presence of a very bad smell.

See DISAPPROVAL B (p. 38) for another gesture used to indicate a bad smell.

SNOBBISHNESS

A.

COMMON.   Chin is lifted several inches; eyes are often partially closed.

SNOBBISHNESS

B.

U.S.   One hand is raised, palm facing away from performer. Head is tilted. Eyes are half closed and lips pursed.

Both SNOBBISHNESS A & B are used to describe referents.

STAND

COMMON. Fingers held together, palm up, hand is extended and moved up and down several times. A command.

STINGINESS

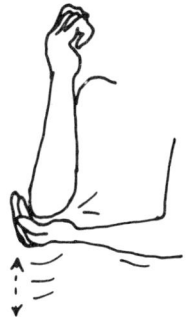

COL. Cupped hand, or fist, strikes bent elbow several times in succession.

Tacaño. (Stingy).

STOP   (Vehicles)
A.

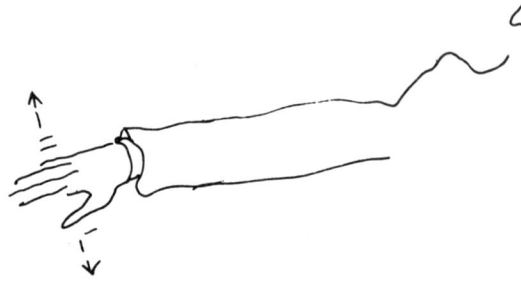

COL.   Arm is outstretched, palm facing down. Fingers, hand or arm may be moved up and down.

STOP
B.

U.S.   Hand with fingers spread moves quickly from side to side.

STOP
C.

COMMON.   Hand is raised, fingers extended together, palm facing oncoming traffic.

STOP
D.

COL.   Policeman places his body at right angles to the oncoming traffic.

STRENGTH
A.

COL.   Performer takes hold of his belt (or garment at the waist) and moves it up and down several times. Male.

HANDBOOK OF GESTURES 133

STRENGTH

B.

COMMON. With arm bent at the elbow, forearm is held parallel to height of body. Hand makes a fist.

STRENGTH

C.

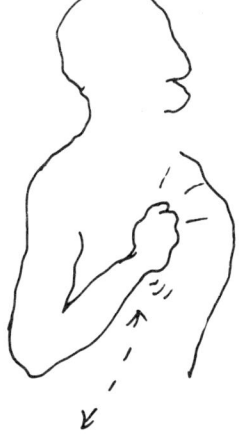

COMMON. One or both fists strike chest several times.

SUCCESS

COMMON. Tip of index finger touches tongue and then makes an imaginary figure one (1) in the air. Used to indicate that the speaker has said something particularly effective, clever or funny.

SURPRISE
A. (Mild)

COMMON. Head is titled or turned, and eyebrows raised.

SURPRISE
B.

COL. Cheeks fill with air and eyebrows are raised.
Que raro! (*How strange!*) often follows.

SURPRISE
C. (Puzzlement)

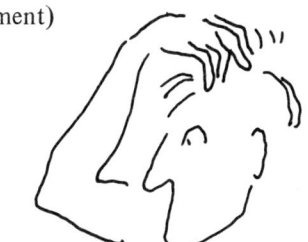

COMMON. Head is scratched, eyebrows raised and lips often pursed. More frequent in U.S.

SURPRISE
D. (Amazement)

U.S. Eyebrows raised. Eyes fully open. Mouth open.

SURPRISE
E.

U.S. Same as SURPRISE D but hands, fingers extended, are placed on cheeks.

TALK (Chatterbox)

    COMMON. Hand is held at face level; fingers and thumb opposed, are moved up and down imitating movement of jaws in talking.

    Chatterbox. Parlanchín.

TELEPHONE
    A.

    COL. Fist rotates by the side of the ear, as if turning a handle.

TELEPHONE
    B.

    COMMON. Hands, with fist closed, as if grasping a French telephone receiver, held near ear.

TERMINATION

A.   (Romance)

COL.   A kick. Not made in the presence of the former partner.

TERMINATION

B.   (Finished)

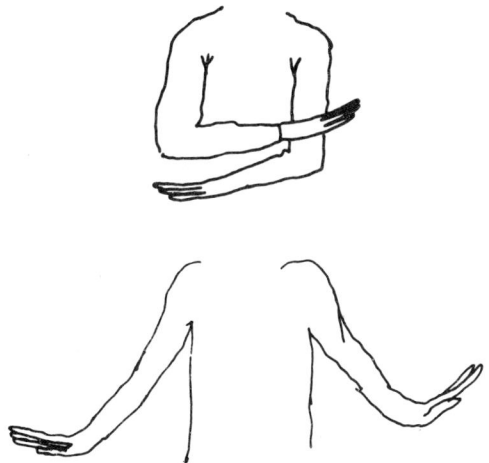

COMMON.   Arms held crossed in front of body, palms down. Then arms move out to the sides. While this gesture often indicates the completion of an action (as in a sports event or a mechanical process) it may also serve as a general negation.

THIEF

COL.   One hand, slightly cupped, scrapes cheek slightly.

THIN

COL.   Little finger is extended vertically from fist.

THOUGHT

A.

COMMON. One hand grasps the elbow or rests in the armpit of the other, while the other hand rests against the side of the chin.

THOUGHT

B.

COL. Hands out to the sides, fingers and thumbs rubbing together.

THOUGHT
    C.

    COMMON.   Thumb and index finger grasp chin.

THOUGHT
    D.

    COMMON.   Thumb is under chin and index finger lies along cheek. This gesture and THOUGHT C are often accompanied by brow wrinkling and eye narrowing.

                THOUGHT C and D have many variations in which various parts of the hand may touch face or head.

HANDBOOK OF GESTURES 141

THOUGHT

E.

U.S.   Heels of the palms are rubbed together repeatedly as hands are firmly clasped. Fingers may be interlocked. Indicates extreme concern or preoccupation.

THOUGHT

F.

U.S.   Index finger, or index plus middle finger, touches lower lip. At times, all fingers may rest on lower lip.

142   HANDBOOK OF GESTURES

THOUGHT

    G.

    COMMON.   Tips of fingers touch in front of (or at) lips or chin.

                   Gestures of THOUGHT may also indicate UNCERTAINTY and WORRY.

THREAT   (of castigation)

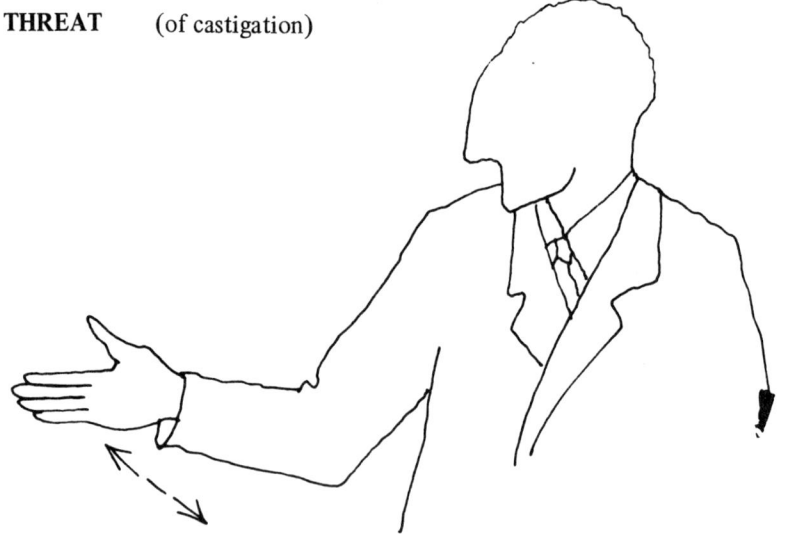

    COL.   With arm bent at elbow and palm up, forearm moves back and forth toward the person threatened. Used by adult to child.

              See WARNING (pp. 147-149).

TIME

   A.

   COMMON.   Index finger taps wrist.

TIME

   B.

   COMMON.   Glance at the wrist.

TIME A & B may signal a request for the time or that it is time ot leave. TIME B is almost always perceived as a signal that the performer is bored, or tired, or wants to terminate the meeting.

TIREDNESS

COMMON. One hand, fingers extended, palm facing body, moves slowly across brow, or across eyes.

Many simulations of relaxed posture (slouches, knee-bends, etc.) are also used to signal tiredness in both cultures. In addition, in the U.S., exaggerated breathing, with mouth wide open and tongue protruding is a common signal for exhaustion.

HANDBOOK OF GESTURES 145

VICTORY

A.

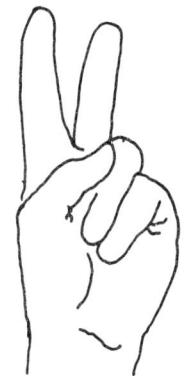

VICTORY

B.

COMMON.   Raised hand clasp. At head level or over head.

WAIT
A.

COMMON. Fingers are normally together, and hand is stationary.

Wait for me. Esperame.

WAIT
B.

U.S. Fingers are often separated, and arm usually moves from side to side.

WARNING
A.

COL. Finger touches cheek just below eye; then arm is extended as finger points at object of or in the direction of danger.

Watch out for . . . . .   *Tén cuidado con .....*

WARNING
B.

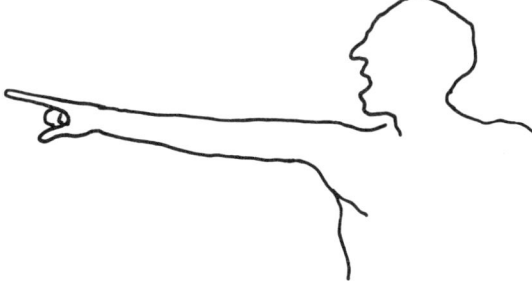

COMMON. In both the United States and Colombia, the extended arm with finger pointing is used to indicate danger of an extraordinary event. Whole arm may be agitated.

148   HANDBOOK OF GESTURES

WARNING
   C.

   COMMON.   Hand, fingers extended and palm facing away from body, is raised in front of body often above head level. Sometimes hand is waved rapidly.

WARNING
   D.

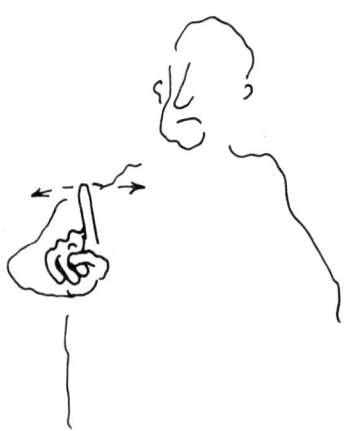

   COL.   Index finger, extended, moves from side to side. Familiar to some informants in U.S.

HANDBOOK OF GESTURES 149

WARNING

E.

U.S.   Index finger extended from fist moves backwards and forwards in the direction of the person being warned. Used most commonly to admonish children.

See SHAME (p. 123).

WHAT?

COMMON.   Hand is cupped behind ear.

What did you say? Como?

WHAT HAPPENED?
A.

COMMON. Hands, palm up, are held out to the sides. Shoulders usually hunch slightly and lips may purse. Much more common in Colombia.

WHAT HAPPENED?
B.

COL. Palm up, hand horizontal to ground. Hand is held out in front of the body and the chin and eyebrows may be raised.

What happened? Qúe pasó?

HANDBOOK OF GESTURES

YES / NO

YES
   A.

   COMMON.   Head is nodded up and down.

NO
   B.

   COL.   Index finger moves from side to side.

NO
   C.

   COMMON.   Head moves from side to side.

SELECTED BIBLIOGRAPHY

Allport, G.W. and Vernon P. *Studies in Expressive Movement* (New York: Macmillan, 1933).
Alsop, Stewart, "How to Speak French Without Saying a Word," *The Saturday Evening Post,* Vol. 233 (December 24-31, 1960), 26-29.
Andrew, Richard J., "Evolution of Facial Expression," *Science* (Nov. 22, 1963), 1034-1041.
— , "The Origin of Facial Expressions," *Scientific American,* Vol. 213, No. 4 (October 1965).
Appel, Victor H., Lawrence T. McCarron, and Bradley A. Manning, "Eyeblink Rate: Behavioral Index of Threat?", *Journal of Counseling Psychology* Vol. 15, No. 2, (1968), 153-157.
Argyle, Michael, *The Psychology of Interpersonal Behavior* (Baltimore Md: Penguin Books, 1967).
Argyle, Michael and Janet Dean, "Eye Contact, Distance and Affiliation," *Sociomatry*, Vol. XXVIII (September 1965), 289-304.
Argyle, Michael and Adam Kendon, "The Experimental Analysis of Social Performance," *Advances in Experimental Psychology,* Vol. 3 (1967).

Bacon, A.M., *A Manual of Gesture* (Chicago, 1873).
Bateson, G. and M. Mead, *Balinese Character: A Photographic Analysis* (New York: Academy of Sciences, 1942).
Bateson, Gregory, "Why do Fenchmen? ", *The Use and Misuse of Language,* S.I. Hayakawa, ed. (New York: Fawcett World Library, 1966), 187-191.
Bateson, Mary Catherine, "Linguistics in the Semiotic Frame," *Linguistics,* Vol. 39 (May 1968).
Baxter, James C., Elaine P. Winters, and R.E. Hammer, "Gestural Behavior During a Brief Interview as a Function of Cognitive Variables," *Journal of Pers. Soc. Psychology,* Vol. 8 (1968), 303-307.
Benesh, Marijana, E. Kramer, and H. Lane, "Recognition of Portrayed Emotion in a Foreign Language," *Experimental Analysis of the Control of Speech*

Production and Perception: III (Ann Arbor, Michigan: University of Michigan Office of Research Administration, 1963).

Berne, Eric, *Games People Play* (New York: Grove Press, Inc., 1964).

Birdwhistell, Ray L., "Background to Kinesics." *ETC. A Review of General Semantics,* Vol. 8 (1956).

—, "Communication Without Words," *L'Aventure Humaine: Encyclopedie des Sciences de l'Homme,* Vol. 5 (Paris: France, 1968), 157-166.

—, "The Contribution of Linguistic-Kinesic Studies to the Understanding of Schizophrenia," *Schizophrenia: An Integrated Approach,* Alfred Auerback, ed. (New York: Ronald Press, 1959), 93-123.

—, "The Frames in the Communication Process." Paper presented to the American Society of Clinical Hypnosis (October •10, 1959), 1-17. (Processed.)

—, *Introduction to Kinesics: An Annotation for Analysis of Body Motion and Gesture* (Washington: Foreign Service Institute, Department of State, 1952).

—, "The Kinetic Level in the Investigation of Emotions," *Expression of Emotions in Man,* Peter H. Knapp, ed. (New York: International Universities Press, Inc., 1963), 123-139.

—, "Kinesics," *International Encyclopedia of the Social Sciences,* Vol 8 (1968), 379-385.

—, "Kinesics and Communication," *Explorations in Communication: An Anthology,* edited by Edmund Carpenter and Marshall McLuhan (Boston: Beacon Press, 1954), 54-64.

—, *Kinesics in Context* (Philadelphia: University of Pennsylvania Press, 1970).

—, "Paralanguage: 25 Years after Sapir," *Lectures on Experimental Psychiatry,* edited by Henry W. Brosin (Pittsburgh: University of Pittsburgh Press, 1961), 43-63.

—, "Some Body Motion Elements Accompanying Spoken American English." Paper presented to the Second International Symposium on Communication Theory and Research, March 23-26, 1966. Published in *Communication: Concepts and Perspectives,* Lee Thayer, ed. (Washington D.C.: Spartan Book, 1967), 53-76.

*Blake, William, *A Preliminary Study of Interpretation of Bodily Expression* (New York: Rumford Press, 1933).

*Bolinger, Dwight, "Thoughts on 'Yep' and 'Nope'," *American Speech,* XXI (1946), 90-95.

Brault , Gerand J., "Kinesics and the Classroom," *French Review,* Vol. 36 (1962), 374-382.

*Brewer, W.D., "Patterns of Gesture Among the Levantine Arabs," *American Anthropologist,* LIII, 232-235.

Burling, Robbins, *Man's Many Voices: Language in its Cultural Context* (New York: Holt, Rinehart, and Winston, Inc., 1970).

*Chase, Stuart, "The Language of Nods," *Saturday Review,* LX (March 2, 1957), 17-18.
Condon, William S., "Process in Communication." Unpublished manuscript, Western Psychiatric Institute and Clinic, Pittsburgh, Pa., July 1964.
— , "Progress Report." Western Psychiatric Institute, Pittsburgh, Pa., 1965. (Mimeographed.)
— , "Synchrony Units and the Communicational Hierarchy." Unpublished manuscript, Western Psychiatric Institute, Pittsburgh, Pa., October, 1963. (Mimeographed.)
Condon, William S. and W.D. Ogston, "A Segmentation of Behavior," *Journal of Psychiatric Research,* 5 (1967), 221-235.
— , "Soundfilm Analysis of Normal and Pathalogical Behavior Patterns," *Journal of Nervous Mental Disorders,* 143 (1966), 338-347.
— , "Speech and Body Motion Synchrony of the Speaker-Hearer." Unpublished paper, Western Psychiatric Institute, Pittsburgh, Pa., January 1968.
Critchley, Macdonald, "Kinesics: Gestural and Mimic Language; An Aspect of Non-verbal Communication," Lipman Halpern, ed. *Problems of Dynamic Neurology: An International Volume. Studies on the Higher Functions of the Human Nervous System* (Jerusalem: Hebrew University, 1963), 181-200.
— , *The Language of Gesture* (London: Edward Arnold, 1939).
Crystal, G. David and Randolph Quirk, *Systems of Prosodic and Paralinquistic Features in English* (The Hague: Mouton, 1964).

Darwin, Charles, *Expression of the Emotion in Man and Animals* (New York: Philosophical Library, 1955).
Davidson, Levette J., "Some Current Folk Gestures and Sign Languages," *American Speech,* XXV (February 1950), 3-9.
Davis, Flora, "How to Read Body Language," *Glamour,* Vol. 62, No. 1 (September 1969).
— , "The Way We Speak 'Body Language'," *The New York Times Magazine* (May 31, 1970), Section 6, p. 8.
Deutsch, Felix, "Analysis of Postural Behavior," *Psychoanalytical Quarterly,* 16 (1947), 192-213.
— , "Analytic Posturology," *Psychoanalytic Quarterly,* 21 (1952), 196-214.
*Diebold, Richard, "Anthropology and the Comparative Psychology of Communicative Behavior," *Animal Communication,* Thomas Sebeok, ed. (Bloomington: Indiana University Press, 1967).
— , "A Survey of Psycholinguistic Research, 1954-64," *Psycholinguistics,* Charles E. Osgood and Thomas A. Sebeok, ed. (Bloomington: Indiana University Press, 1965), 205-291.
Donohue, H.E.F., "Where Should You Touch?", *Eye Magazine* (Sept. 1968), pp. 27-8, 82-3.

Efron, David, *Gesture and Environment* (New York: King's Crown Press, 1941).
Ekman, Paul, "Body Position, Facial Expression & Verbal Behavior," *Journal of Abnormal and Social Psychology*, LXVIII, 3 (1964).
—, "Communication Through Nonverbal Behavior." Progress Report, University of California, Langley Porter Institute, San Francisco, California, 1965. (Mimeographed.)
—, "Differential Communication of Affect by Head and Body Cues," *Journal of Personality and Social Psychology*, 2 (1965), 726-735.
Ekman, Paul and W.V. Friesen, "The Analysis and Classification of Filmed Acts." Unpublished manuscript, Langley Porter, San Francisco, California, 1965. (Mimeographed).
—, "Nonverbal Behavior in Psychotherapy Research," *Research on Psychotherapy*, J. Shlien, ed., APA, III (1967).
—, "Origin, Usage and Coding: The Basis of Five Categories of Nonverbal Behavior." Paper given at the Symposium: "Communication Theory and Linguistic Models in the Social Sciences" at the Center for Social Research at the Torpcuato Di Tella Institute, Buenos Aries, Argentina, October, 1967.
—, "VID-R and Scan: Tools and Methods for the Automated Analysis of Visual Records." Unpublished manuscript, Langley Porter, San Francisco, California, 1968. (Mimeographed.)

Feldman, S., *Mannerisms of Speech and Gestures in Everyday Life*, Part 2 (New York: International Universities Press, 1959).
Frank, Lawrence, "Tactile Communication," *Explorations in Communication*, Edmund Carpenter and Marshall McLuhan, eds. (Boston: Beacon Press, 1960), 4-11.

Geldard, Frank, "Body English," *Psychology Today*, II, 7 (1968).
—, "Cutaneous Channels of Communications", *Sensory Communication*, Wiley, ed. (1961).
—, "Some Neglected Possibilities of Communication," *Science*, 131 (1960), 1585-1588.
"Gesture Language," *Life*, XXVIII (January 9, 1950), 79-82.
Goffman, Erving, *Behavior in Public Places* (Glencoe, Ill.: The Free Press of Glencoe, 1963).
—, *Encounters: Two Studies in the Sociology of Interaction* (Indianapolis, Indiana: Bobbs-Merrill Co., 1961).
—, *The Presentation of Self in Everyday Life* (Edinburgh: University of Edinburgh, 1956).
Green, Jerald R., *A Gesture Inventory for the Teaching of Spanish* (New York: Chilton Books, 1968).
Gumperz, John J., and Dell Hymes, eds., *The Ethnography of Communication.*

Menasha Wisc.: American Anthropological Association. *American Anthropologist*, Special Publication, Vol. 66, No. 6, Part 2, (December, 1964).

Hall, Edward T., *The Silent Language* (Garden City, N.Y.: Doubleday, 1959).
Hayes, Francis C., "Gesture," *Encyclopedia Americana*, XII (1966), 627a-627d.
— , "Should We Have A Dictionary of Gestures?", *Southern Folklore Quarterly*, IV (1940), 239-245.
— , "Gesture: A Working Bibliography," *Southern Folklore Quarterly*, XXI (December, 1957), 218-317.
Hewes, Gordon W., "The Anthropology of Posture," *Scientific American*, CXCVI (Feb., 1957), 122-132.
— , "The Domain Posture," *Anthropological Linguistics*, VIII, 8 (Nov., 1966), 106-112.
— , "World Distribution of Certain Postural Habits," *American Anthropologist*, 57 (1955), 231-244.
Holiday (April, 1960), 112.
Hymes, Dell, *Language in Culture and Society* (New York: Harper & Row, 1964).

Jablonko, Allison, "Dance and Daily Activities Among the Maring People of New Guinea: A Cinematographic Analysis of Body Movement Style." Unpublished Ph.D. dissertation, Columbia University, 1968.
Joos, Martin, *The Five Clocks* (New York: Harcourt Brace and World, 1967).

Kaplan, Edith, "Gestural Representation of Implement Usage: An Organismic-Developmental Study," Unpublished dissertation, Clark University, 1968.
Kaulfers, Walter Vincent, "Curiosities of Colloquial Gesture," *Hispania*, XIV (October, 1931), 249-264.
Kendon, Adam, "Movement Coordination in Social Interaction: Some Examples Described," *Acta Psychologica*, 32 (1970), 100-125.
— , "Some Functions of Gaze-direction in Social Interaction," *Acta Psychologica*, 26 (1967), 22-63.
— , "Some Relationships Between Body Motion and Speech: An Analysis of an Example," *Studies in Dyadic Interaction*, A. Siegman and B. Pope, eds. (New York: Pergamon Press, 1970).
King, William, "Hand Gestures," *Western Folklore*, VIII (1949), 13-14.
Krout, Maurice H., "Understanding Human Gesture," *Scientific Monthly*, XLIX (August, 1939), 167-172.

LaBarre, Weston, "The Cultural Basis of Emotions and Gestures," *Journal of Personality*, XVI (September, 1947), 49-68.
— , "Paralinguistics, Kinesics, and Cultural Anthropology," *Approaches to Semiotics*, Thomas A. Sebeok, Alfred S. Hayer, and Mary Catherine Bateson, eds. (The Hague: Mouton and Company, 1964), 191-220.

Lamb, Warren, *Posture and Gesture* (London: Gerald Duckworth & Co. Ltd., 1965).
Lamb, Warren & David Turner, *Management Behavior* (New York: International Universities Press, 1969).
Leeb, F., "The Fist." Unpublished manuscript, Western Psychiatric Institute, Pittsburgh, Pa., 1967.
Lomax, Alan, *Folk Song Style and Culture* (Washington, D.C.: American Association for the Advancement of Science, 1968).

Madariaga, S. de, *Englishmen, Frenchmen, Spaniards* (London: Oxford, 1928).
Mahl, G., B. Danet, and N. Norton, "Reflection of Major Personality Characteristics in Gestures and Body Movements," *American Psychologist*, XIV (1959), 357.
Mathieu, G., "Pitfalls of Pattern Practice (Gestures)," *Modern Language Journal*, Vol. 48 (1964), 20-24.
McQuown, Norman A., ed., *Natural History of An Interview* (Forthcoming).
Meerlo, Joost A.M., *Unobtrusive Communication: Essays in Psycholinguistics* (Assen, The Netherlands: Van Gorcum, Ltd., 1964).
Mehrabian, Albert, "Communication Without Words," *Psychology Today*, II, 4 (Sept., 1968).
—, "Orientation Behaviors and Nonverbal Attitude Communication," *Journal of Communication*, 17, 4 (December, 1967), 324-332.
*Morris, Charles W., *Signs, Language and Behavior* (New York, 1946).
Mosher, Joseph A., *The Essentials of Effective Gesture* (New York: MacMillian Co., 1916).

Osgood, C.E. & A.W. Heyer, Jr., "Objective Studies in Meaning II. The Validity of Posed Facial Expressions as Gestural Signs in Interpersonal Communication," *American Psychologist*, Vol. (1950), 298 — .
Ott, Edward, *How to Gesture* (New York: Hinds and Noble, 1892).

Pike, Kenneth L., *Language: In Relation to a Unified Theory of the Structure of Human Behavior* (Glendale, California: Summer Institute of Linguistics, Part I, 1954, Part II, 1955, Part III, 1960).
—, "Toward a Theory of the Structure of Human Behavior," *Language in Culture and Society*, Dell Hymes, ed. (New York: Harper and Row, 1964), 54-62.
Pittenger, Robert E., Charles F. Hockett, and John Danehy, *The First Five Minutes: A Sample of Miscroscopic Interview Analysis* (Ithaca, New York: Paul Martineau, 1960).

Ruesch, Jurgen and Gregory Bateson, *Communication. The Social Matrix of Psychiatry* (New York: W.W. Norton and Company, Inc., 1951).

Ruesch, Jurgen and Weldon, Kees, *Nonverbal Communication: Notes On The Visual Perception of Human Relations* (Berkeley: University of California Press, 1956).
— , *Nonverbal Communication* (Berkeley and Los Angeles: University of California Press, 1964).

Saitz, Robert and Edward Cervenka, *Colombian and North American Gestures* (Bogota: Centro Colombo-Americano, 1962).
Saturday Review, XL, 9 (March 2, 1957).
Scheflen, Albert E., "Behavioral Programs in Human Communication," *General Systems Theory and Psychiatry,* W. Gray, F. Dahl, & N. Rizzo, eds. (New York: Little, Brown, 1969).
— , "Communication and Regulation in Psychotherapy," *Psychiatry,* 26 (1963), 126-136.
— , "Quasi-Courting Behavior in Psycho-Therapy," *Psychiatry,* 28 (1965), 245-257.
—, "The Significance of Posture in Communication Systems," *Psychiatry,* 27 (1964), 316-331.
— , *Stream and Structure of Communicational Behavior. Behavioral Studies Monograph No. 1* (Eastern Pennsylvania Psychiatric Institute, Commonwealth of Pennsylvania, 1965).
— , "Systems in Human Communication." Paper presented at the Meetings of the American Association for the Advancement of Science, University of California, Berkeley, Calif., 1965. (Mimeographed).
Schnapper, Melvin. "Your Actions Speak Louder," *Peace Corps Volunteer* (June, 1969), 7-10.
Sebeok, Thomas, Afred Hayes, and Mary Catherine Bateson, *Approaches to Semiotics.* (The Hague: Mouton & Co., 1964).
Smith, Frank and George Miller, *The Genesis of Language* (Cambridge M.I.T. Press, 1966).
Smith, Henry Lee, Jr., "Language and the Total System of Communication," *Linguistics Today,* Archibald A. Hill, ed. (New York: Basic Books, Inc., 1969), 89-102.

Thompson, D.F. & L. Meltzer, "Communication of Emotional Intent by Facial Expression," *Journal of Abnormal and Social Psychology,* Vol., (1964), 129-135.
Time, 70, 3 (July 15, 1957).
— , 85, 15 (April 9, 1969).
Trager, George L., "Paralanguage: A First Approximation," *Language in Culture and Society,* Dell Hymes, ed. (New York: Harper and Row, 1964), 274-288.
— , "Toas III: Paralanguage," *Anthropological Linguistics,* II, 2, 24-30.

—, "The Typology of Paralanguage," *Anthropological Linguistics*, III, I (1961) 17-21.

Trager, George L., and Edward Hall, *The Analysis of Culture* (Washington, D.C. Foreign Service Institute, 1953).

Vogue, 138, 1 (July, 1961).

SOURCES RELATED TO PROXEMICS

Ames, R.G., et al., "Sex Differences in Social Distance," *Sociology and Social Research*, Vol. 52 (April, 1968), 280-289.

Bogardus, E.S., "The Measurement of Social Distance," *Readings in Social Psychology* (New York: Henry Holt & Co., 1947), Section XII.

"Definitions of: 'Social Distance,'" *A Dictionary of the Social Sciences*, The Free Press of Glencoe. Compiled by UNESCO, 1964.

Engebretson, D., "Crosscultural Variations in Territoriality: A Base-line Determination of Interactional Distance Between Shared Culture Dyads." Unpublished doctoral dissertation, University of Hawaii, 1969.

Hall, Edward T., *The Hidden Demension* (Garden City, N.Y.: Doubleday, 1966).
Horowitz, J.B., S.F. Duff, and Lois O. Stratton, "Body-buffer zone: Exploration of personal space," *Archives of General Psychiatry* (1964), II, 651-656.
—, "A system for the Notation of Proxemic Behavior," *American Anthropologist*, 65, 5 (October, 1963), 1003-1026.

Just, Lee R., "A Study of Mennonite Social Distance Reactions," *Sociology and Social Research*. Vol. 38, (March-April, 1954), 222-226.

Landis, Judson R., et. al., "Race and Social Class as Determinants of Social Distance," *Journal of Applied Sociology*, Vol. 51 (October, 1966), 78-86.

Little, K.B., "Personal Space," *Journal of Experimental Social Psychology*, 1 (1965), 237-247.

Opara, P.A.V., "Social Distance Attitude of Nigerian Students," *Phylon*, Vol. XXIX (Spring, 1968), 13-18.

Poole, Williard C., Jr., "Social Distance and Personal Distance," *Journal of Applied Sociology*, Vol. XI (Sept.-Oct., 1926), 114-120.

Scheflen, Albert E., "Human Territoriality in Home and Neighborhood," NIH Grant Proposal No. MH 15977-01 (xeroxed).
Schwartz, Barry, "The Social Psychology of Privacy," *The American Journal of Sociology*, Vol. 13 (May, 1968), 741-752.
Sommer, Robert, "Studies in Personal Space," *Sociometry*, 22 (1959), 247-260.
– , "Sociofugal Space," *American Journal of Sociology*, Vol. LXXII (May, 1967), 654-660.
– , "The Distance for Comfortable Conversation: A Further Study," *Sociometry*, 25 (1962), 111-125.
Sommer, R., and N.J. Felipe, "Invasions of Personal Space," *Social Problems*, Vol. XIV (Fall, 1966), 206-214.

SOURCES RELATED TO KINESICS AND TEACHING

Brault, Gerard J., "Kinesics and the Classroom: Some Typical French Gestures," *The French Review*, XXXVI (February, 1963), 374-382.
Brooks, Nelson, "Teaching Culture in the Foreign Language Classroom," *Foreign Language Annals*, I (March, 1968), 204-217.

Galas, Evangeline M., "The Language Teacher as Choral Director: Suggestions on Use of Gestures," *Hispania*, XLIV (December, 1961), 787-789.

Hayes, Alfred S., "Paralinguistics and Kinesics: Pedagogical Perspectives," *Approaches to Semiotics* Thomas A. Sebeok, Aflred S. Hayes, and Mary Catherine Bateson, eds. (The Hague: Mouton & Co., 1964), 145-172.

Saitz, Robert L., "Gestures in the Classroom," *English Language Teaching*, Vol. 21 (1) (1966), 33-37.

WORD INDEX

admonish, 149
agreement, 15
amazement, 135
anger, 16, 17
anticipation, 17, 18, 21
applause, 21
approbation, 20
approval, 18, 19, 20, 21
ask, 105
assent, 15
attention, 21, 22, 23
aversion, 23

baby, 24
beautiful, 19
belittlement, 41
bet, 24
bored, 143
boredom, 25, 74
bow, 67
breasts, 122
burning, 25

castigation, 73, 142
chagrin, 46, 100
chatterbox, 136
check, 108, 109
cigarette, 25
cold, 26
come, 27, 28
completion, 137
complication, 29
concern, 141
conviviality, 55
cross, 29
crowd, 30
cuckold, 121

dance, 30
danger, 50, 147
delicacy, 31
denial, 32, 33, 37
directions, 33, 34, 35
disagreement, 36
disappointment, 37
disapproval, 38
disbelief, 39-42
discomfort, 72
disgust, 43
disinterest, 43
disparagement, 41
drink, 44, 45
drunk, 45

emphasis, 46, 47
encouragement, 48
enthusiasm, 49
excitement, 50
exhaustion, 144

fat, 51
faux pas, 51, 52
favor, 53
female, 54
fight, 17, 54
fine, 31
flirtation, 20, 55
following, 55
food, 56, 57, 58, 71
forgetfulness, 46
forgetting, 86
friendliness, 55
friendship, 57
frustration, 58
full, 58

give, 89, 104
go, 59, 60
goad, 60
goodbye, 27, 61, 62, 63
good looking, 19
gossip, 64
graft, 64
greetings, 65-69

handshake, 24, 61
hat, 67, 68
height, 70
hello, 63
hitchhiking, 70
homosexual, 119, 120
hot, 71, 72
hungry, 57

impatience, 73, 74
imprisonment, 74
insanity, 75
insults, 76, 77
intelligence, 78
intercourse, 116, 117
invitation, 20, 30

kiss, 79

leave, 80, 81
lesbian, 121
lizard, 83
luck, 82, 83

marriage, 83, 84
masculinity, 85
masturbation, 122
me, 113

WORD INDEX

memory, 86, 87
money, 88, 89, 90
more or less, 92

negation, 137
nervousness, 92
no, 151
no information, 92, 93
nothing, 33

oath, 94

pay, 89
perfection, 21, 95
phallic, 114, 115
photograph, 95
picture, 95
policeman, 59, 126, 131
preoccupation, 141
pride, 96, 97
prostitute, 118
protection, 29
proximity, 97
punishment, 98
puzzlement, 135

quickly, 99

recognition, 99
regret, 100, 101, 102
remembering, 86, 87

repetition, 103
requests, 104, 105
restaurant, 106, 110
retribution, 111
revenge, 111
review, 112
romance, 137

saintliness, 112
salute, 69
secret, 123
self, 113
sexual, 114-122
sexually attractive, 19
shame, 123
silence, 123
sit, 124
sleep, 125
slow down, 126
small, 126
smell, 127
smoking, 25
snobishness, 128
stand, 129
standing, 69
stinginess, 129
stop, 70, 130, 131
strength, 132, 133
success, 134
surprise, 134, 135
swear, 94

table, 108
talk, 136
tasty, 19
telephone, 136
termination, 137
thief, 138
thin, 138
thought, 139-142
threat, 17, 142
time, 143
tiredness, 143, 144
touching, 97
traffic, 59

unreliability, 39

vehicle, 55, 130
victory, 145

wait, 146
waiter, 106, 107
warning, 147, 148
wave, 61
weather, 72
what, 149
what happened, 150
wink, 55
wonderful, 19

yawn, 25
yes, 151